A catalogue record for this book is available from the British Library.

Third edition 2015
ISBN 978-0-9565137-1-7
Published by NR Publishing

Second edition 2010
Published by NR Publishing

First edition 2006
Published by Exposure Publishing

Cover design and photograph by Paul Berryman
www.berryman.ca

For recordings and other publications by Nick Roach Teachings, please visit the website: www.nickroach.co.uk

Essays in Truth

Glimpses into Reality

Nick Roach

Sally Powell

iv

Nick Roach began teaching at the end of 2003, following thirteen years of dedication to a method which is perhaps best described simply as 'self-observation and personal honesty'. Longing for a reason, and even an end, to emotional suffering in his life, all the years of insights and experiences finally came together in the one known by many names including 'Self-Realisation', 'God Realisation' and 'Enlightenment'.

Initially the teaching of this to others began with setting up the website and giving talks at a number of holistic shows in the London area. This soon developed into responding to letters and emails from all over the world from people asking questions and showing appreciation for the simple, down-to-earth style in which Nick teaches.

On this page we would like to display a small portion of the wonderful feedback and comments Nick has received since he began sharing what he has experienced.

Comments

'I loved your website. Your simple words have undeniable power. They have shaken me up! I will use your insights on emotions to deal with the unwelcome experience of poor health that has distracted me for the last year...' UK

'...you are like a radar beacon, reflecting a ship's signal and guiding it on its voyage...' Canada

'When I was talking to you I felt that my mind was becoming so still that I could not think, in fact I could hardly hear what you were saying. I was feeling peaceful and aware but also fearful. I could feel love and felt that I could transform myself or move into something but I chose not to...' UK

'I have gone through the article "Liberation" and I think it is beautifully written. There is a freshness and directness in your approach which is quite unique...' India

'Your method is the most effective I have found for clearing the mind and I have learnt a lot over the past week...' Australia

'You have a refreshing lightness and clarity, and a goodness shines through giving the feeling that everything is in some way all alright...' UK

'Your teaching is more like pure Advaita, which as I said, I am quite familiar with...' UK

'It's always a pleasure to speak with a reflection who fully understands where I'm coming from...' UK

'Thank you for taking the time to create this website and for sharing this teaching so generously. I feel truly blessed...'

Following the publication of his first book, *Enlightenment, the Simple Path*, it was noticed that Nick's website contained more than enough substance to fill another book. Removal of these eighty or so pages would make way for new pages and a new site, and is the source of the majority of this book. Largely the pages are displayed as they were initially written by Nick and Sally (Nick's partner), as they embarked on their web design and publishing adventure, and into the world of teaching the experience that they were living.

Introduction

The contents of this book were written over a period of three years, one page at a time, as the idea for each arose in Nick, and in pretty much the order in which they occur here. Each subject or chapter was published on the website, itself steadily growing in size as time progressed, and the contents of which were never expected to be made into a book such as this. However, they are amazing pieces and describe the process Nick went through as the state deepened in him. You may notice the style changing as you read Nick's words and interact with him in person. This is perhaps particularly apparent in some of the later sections of this book, which could even be said to conflict with the earlier pieces. All were correct at the time, as they were experienced, and serve to demonstrate how the truth moves on. What is true today, no matter how true it seems, may be pushed aside for a greater truth tomorrow. Better to roll with it and enjoy the ride than try to fight it and hold on to old and out-of-date ideas. This also applies to Nick's own relationship within himself with his own Master's teachings, and you will see how Nick begins to look beyond these in his own experience and with his own perspective, no longer simply taking on faith that which he had held on to for so many years, simply because it was what he was taught.

Feel free to dip into this book as you wish, but there is a great story if you read in page order as the journey within unfolds.

Contents

Contents

Contents

Enlightenment

Here are a series of pages looking into this mystical and elusive state of mind called 'Enlightenment'. The content is quite comprehensive, describing a little about my path and a lot of detail about the experience itself as it occurred to me at the time, perhaps six months to a year into the uninterrupted living of the Realisation.

This is often the ultimate question for people on what is commonly referred to as 'the Spiritual Path', a little like the question 'What is the Matrix?' in the film of that name. Here I offer an answer from my own experience. This page was one of the first pages written for the site at the beginning of 2004.

What Is Enlightenment?

Enlightenment is the state of being before the mind creates opinions and beliefs about reality and what it is. The experience of Enlightenment is of being a 'space' of 'intelligence' with no form, no shape, no beginning and no end, and yet it is to be the source of all that is.

Misconceptions and further explanations

It has been said that Enlightenment is to be 'at one with the universe', with little or no explanation as to how this can occur (and many dispute whether it is even possible at all).

In my own experience it began with a sense of peace and a feeling that all is well. I began to see life giving me experiences to help me learn and I frequently witnessed amazing coincidences. I began to see that there really is an intelligence behind this existence.

I lived with this for a while and soon saw that if there is an intelligence behind everything, it must also be behind *me*, as I am a part of 'everything'. This intelligence, whatever it is, has been called God, Allah, Cosmic Consciousness and Universal Mind amongst other things. I began to see that if there is a 'Being' behind everything, I must indeed be a part of it, whatever it is.

I felt exhilarated as it dawned on me that therefore I really am a part of 'God' (or whichever name you choose). I lived with this knowledge for a while, until I was hit with a further insight: If there is one intelligence (one God) behind all existence, then ultimately, not only am I a part of it, but I am it. I am here after all, and all is one. Otherwise I am saying God is everything and then there's me, and

3

that would be silly. There was a terrible fear in this as I began to lose all I thought I was, for ultimately I saw that I really am alone, as God is alone.

In grace, each insight passed leaving only an imprint of knowledge to be slowly absorbed into my experience. For such Self-knowledge to remain constant, before the individual is able to cope with it, would be too much. Soon each insight becomes knowledge and is unquestionable and undeniable.

Life continued as before. Nothing had really changed. I just had more Self-knowledge and saw lessons in situations as they occurred. For me, after years of living with the knowledge that ultimately this being 'I' am (whatever it is) is all there is, I had the experience of actually being alone whilst with people. I was seated talking with another person and suddenly I was talking to myself. The person and all else were part of me, part of this being I am. I continued the conversation with this other part of myself as I knew it must go on, as all goes on. This experience also passed, to return later at various times and eventually to become a constant state after perhaps six months.

So, to me, the experience of 'Enlightenment' is to *be* the only one here (and not just to know it). The knowledge in it is that 'I' (whatever 'I' am) am also the source of all that is, has been and will be, and that nothing exists without me being here. In this there is no past or future, as everything happens now or not at all.

That is why Enlightenment has also been called 'God Realisation'. Not because a man or woman can *be* 'God', but because they are deeply enough in touch with their being that they know it as the one being, as all apparent beings come from the one; *are* the one.

However, life does not end there. The intelligence, God, had a need for existence in the first place. That need is being dissolved with each experience and becomes finer and stiller, detaching further and further from the need to exist and yet enjoying the separate forms while they are present.

This experience and knowledge is available to all who are ready, as it is the source of all things. A person who has 'Realised

4

God' – that is, realised that I, my being, is all there is – is said also to be a 'Spiritual Master', not because s/he is above anybody else, but it would seem to be as good a name as any to describe the experience of being the one being behind all the forms: the Master Consciousness.

There are many ideas as to what a Spiritual Master is and little knowledge as to why you would need one, if you do. This page is to explain a little about the 'Master', in the sense of Enlightenment, and why you do need one if you are to progress to deeper levels.

What Is a Master?

A Spiritual Master is, in my experience, an individual who is in the state of union. That is, within himself or herself, the individual is in a state of not only knowing the being they are is all there is, but is also in the experience as a constant state of really being the only one here, every moment seeing all the environment as merely a reflection of their own being.

Teacher or Master?

You can therefore see from the above that a teacher may not be a Master (and not all Masters teach).

A teacher may have had some experiences and is able therefore to share their knowledge with people, but they themselves still have a way to go to get to the point they are seeking. A Master is at that point. If a Master teaches, it is to reflect totally the being back to the one being taught. The Master can connect the 'seeker' directly with their source, whereas a teacher can only tell the person how to find it according to their own understanding and limited experience.

However, because of the above, the Master may not allow the person any time. The truth is within them now, not next week or next year, and the Master aims to expose this. A teacher is still on the path that they are teaching, so still needs more time, so teaches more time. Enlightenment is *now* and now there is no time. Time happens when the mind is allowed to string situations together. Otherwise there is just being.

So, the answer to the question 'Why do "I" need a Master?' is: because only the Master (and I say 'the' Master not 'a' because the individual realises the one being as his/her own being, and therefore

6

is *the* only one behind all) can reflect the original state to you, instead of telling you about what someone else has said or written.

And will any Master do? First, despite the state being every person's basic nature and the source of their being, there are very few Enlightened beings on the planet at one time. However, one will be there for you when you are ready.

Perhaps, complicating things further, you have the Masters who don't teach, as ultimately they see everyone gets there in the end as all is one, so why bother teaching? This may be true but the Master still has to live, so what better thing to do than to share this knowledge, which is after all the self-knowledge of every person.

Then you have those that do teach, but teach that they have realised God as their own being and therefore encourage people to worship them (the Master). This is not really teaching at all, because unless the Master is teaching the individual how to realise and be it for themselves without needing to follow anyone, what is the point? The point is, of course, just self-gratification on the part of the Master.

Then you have others who teach well, but due perhaps to some enforced doctrine or just self-gratification teach one thing and do another. An example of this is those who have taught the way of celibacy and have been exposed later as not having been celibate at all. Even these are doing their best (as everyone does). The ideal would of course be to find a Master who lives what he teaches and teaches the truth.

So Masters can lie? Of course! In the end a Master is just a person who has united enough with their own being to know the being they are is all there is, and who is living it. There's nothing in there about telling the truth.

So what can you do? All you can do is go with a teaching that seems to suit you best and feels right. Be careful not to 'shop around too much', whether through a lack of commitment or a need for entertainment, while claiming to be searching for the truth. If you find a teaching that works, live it as much as you can. Soon it will be your own truth. The Master will be provided when you are ready, as everything is provided when it is time.

7

Until recently I was of the view that I would welcome any and all people interested in my teaching, and would reply to emails and assist wherever I am able. However, something has changed...

More than One Master?

This page is in two parts: Part One describes the situation of (perhaps doggedly) claiming to follow only one teaching, while at the same time looking to other sources for answers or explanations of the one you follow. Part Two describes the situation of not really following any specific teaching or teacher at all and instead trying to follow all at once.

Part one

I have received correspondence from a number of people who would say they are following another Master's teaching and look to me to either explain how mine fits with theirs, to confirm what they are already doing (and argue if it seems different) or worse, that I explain the other teacher's words as they are unable to approach their teacher personally.

My aim is to provide the simplest, most effective, direct and practical method (and teaching) possible. I am very willing to assist where I am able, anyone with genuine questions as to how to do this, or even just help confirm some of their own experiences. However, if you do follow another Master's teaching and it is not up to the task, at least have the honesty and responsibility and insight to see the existing teaching is not giving you what you need. If you are still seeking answers to questions they do not provide, and if the teacher is unobtainable (either through death, or being 'too busy' or just unapproachable), I suggest you should not look to another teacher to compensate for the inadequacies of the current while still calling them your teacher or Master. A good teacher should not be used as a translation service to compensate for other teachers who are unable or unwilling to explain their own words.

Does this sound harsh? Allow me to put this in perspective for you: As we know, there is a lot of dispute over which teachings work and which is best etc. The truth really is that whatever you are doing at the time must be right for you or you would not be doing it, but just imagine for a moment you are a teacher...

Someone approaches you and says words to the effect of: '*I am a devoted follower of The Truth of the Apple Tree Cult and it is wonderful and I will always be a member of it. However, I want you to answer a number of questions for me. If I don't agree with your answers I will tell you I think you are wrong, because I have been told something different by my beloved cult, and will walk away pleased I have been able to correct you or annoyed that you presume to teach something that is contrary to my own beloved cult. If, however, you do teach me anything, I will not give you any credit as I am a member of The Truth of the Apple Tree Cult and do not follow anybody else. Therefore I will go away and impress others with what I know and claim my cult as the source of my knowledge.*'

Looking at the above, not only is the action dishonest, but it confuses people who are still seeking, because they will actually credit your cult or teaching with some insight of truth which is not deserved, and it thus covers up the inadequacies in the teaching and perpetuates it further.

So, if you call yourself a Buddhist, a Sannyasin, a Christian, a Hindu, a follower of Barry Long or any other teaching or teacher, whether alive or dead, and you are looking for more answers from another teacher who is available while still holding to your current faith, perhaps it's time to have a look at what you are doing(?). Is it time to let go of your past beliefs or ideas, which indeed have served you until now, and move into a new area? Perhaps the old teachings have prepared you for a 'new' way, such as in the story of Siddhartha Gautama where, after years of trying out different teachings, he came to the stillness within where there was 'Nothing arising' and found this was the truth; thus it is said he became the original Buddha (Enlightened One).

9

The truth is the same now as it always was – the stillness within you. Just be aware of where you are and of what you are feeling now! That is the truth. 'You' are the truth! You don't need to follow anybody else. Follow a teaching if it works for you, but don't hold fast to an old or weak teaching through habit, routine, peer pressure, a sense of identity, loyalty or just sheer stubbornness if it is not serving you any more. Be new now. The truth is within you now and that is where you will find it.

Part two

Having said all the above, we then have many who are still 'window shopping' and are not with any specific teacher or teaching at all. There may indeed be some desire in them to find the truth, but with all the different Masters, teachers and teachings, they have missed the point.

We receive many emails from people expressing sentiments such as, 'I have been reading a book by (insert name) and he said '............', which I really liked. It reminded me of (insert name) when he said '............', which is similar to when you say '............'. I have also read the book by (insert name) who said '............', which seems to be the same but in a different way. Then there is (insert name) who said '............', which seems contradictory to when you say '............' and when (insert name) says '............'. What I don't understand is how to fit this all together? Can you help?'

The answer to the question is, of course, not to try! Don't try to fit the words of different teachers together. You will get confused. It's hard enough to get to grips with one Master when he is speaking of things beyond the comprehension of the thinking mind. Each Master is experiencing the truth as a living experience (if he is). This must then be translated into words to be expressed for another mind to translate back again, but into something different as the words were trying to describe the experience to a person not in it. This alone is a recipe for confusion, if not disaster, without trying to fit together several different descriptions from different sources of the same thing...

10

So (and this has been said before) it is best to find one teaching that feels true to you, one that has the 'ring of truth' and seems to work in your own experience, and live it to the best of your ability. Any teaching that is true, I suggest, will be advising you to 'feel the space where you are', or 'be aware that you exist', or whatever way this is described in that teaching. No amount of analysing, reading, talking or thinking is going to lead you to the truth. It just tells you about it and gives you more to think about.

I will say it again here now so you are under no misconception as to what or where the truth is: The space you can feel inside you at this moment, the awareness you have when you are aware that you exist, IS THE TRUTH! And the more you feel and are aware of it, the more you become it. You can read a thousand books a week telling you this in different ways and in different languages, but until you actually do it yourself, it is just entertainment (not that there is anything wrong with that, but it's good to be aware if that's all you are doing).

If you like the sound of what's in these pages, you may be wondering how to do it. There are stories of Eastern Masters living in caves or sitting in painful looking positions for hours on end. Neither of these are requirements to attaining this state.

The Way to Enlightenment

Before we look at the way to Enlightenment, we need to know what it is heading to. That is to ask, what does it mean?

Put simply, Enlightenment is not wanting anything beyond what is now. Any emotional wants or trying must be let go of. This means not wanting something beyond what is here now and yet still operating effectively in this world without having to withdraw to a cave or monastery, as the Eastern Masters have in the past.

The fact is, everything is created by *the* being, your being, so everything is within you already. You cannot realise this (make this real in your own experience) while you allow yourself to think about and imagine what is not, as this separates you from the knowledge that you are complete and therefore you feel incomplete. So how do you stop thinking? You think because you are emotional. You are emotional because you think. It is indeed a circle where one feeds the other.

When something happens to make you unhappy, you feel the emotion. The emotion drives your mind to re-live the situation over and over, like a movie that has got stuck. You are stuck in time and that separates you from the moment, from your feeling of being complete. The more you think, the more emotion you feel, and the more emotion you feel, the more you think. This is the process in every emotional un-Enlightened mind, and it goes on your entire life.

What happens is this: Every time you are emotional and thus separate yourself from feeling complete, you feed the emotion by thinking about the situation which caused the emotion, thus making it stronger. The emotion, once the situation has passed, does not

12

disappear as we seem to think. It goes into the psyche, into the being, which is your being. Over time it grows and becomes a constant discomfort from which there seems to be little peace, always ready to pounce into action should it see any reason to react. It would defend your body if there was a need but there usually isn't for most of us, so we use it to defend our emotional self, to control others and to fight for our right to feel the way we do, and to be unhappy when we feel it is justified or just when it suits. We will blame everyone else for how bad we feel and yet justify our right to feel that way. This is dishonest and unacceptable and yet the whole world accepts it.

Lesson 1

The first lesson is perhaps to give up holding on to your <u>right</u> to be unhappy. Stop blaming others for your life and how you feel!

Sure, if someone hurts you physically, you must react to defend yourself (your body) and take appropriate action. They are indeed responsible for what they did to you (until you learn you are responsible for your whole life), but you are still responsible for how you *feel about it*. While you blame another for your feelings, you are stuck with them: trapped in a self-imposed prison to which only you have the key; and the key is to accept responsibility for everything you feel. In practice this means when the feeling comes up from a situation that makes you emotional, you will first find yourself drawn into it. It is here that you need to bring your attention back to the situation, back to the moment, to your awareness of your body where you are complete.

You must first look to see if there is anything practical that can be done to improve the situation. You will never be able to rest while there is some action you feel you should take but choose not to. Also, accept that while there may be nothing that can be done right now, there may be something you can do later, so don't panic.

Once you have looked at the situation (and I mean looked *at*, not gone round in circles thinking *about*), and you have done everything you can see that can be done at this time, regardless of any fear there may be of taking the action, then the work starts.

The work is to dissolve the emotion rather than feeding it. This is done by simply holding the knowledge of the problem in your awareness (you will get the hang of this quickly) and resisting the force of the emotion and its attempts to take you away and dive into the emotional world of your imagination. As you hold the knowledge of the problem, you will feel the emotion very strongly pulling and pushing from various sides in your mind, to make you think and lose yourself. If you do give in you will be feeding the emotion, only to make it stronger for when it comes again next time. Be aware, though, that it does behave like a living entity and is very clever. While you are holding the knowledge of the problem (and really pleased with yourself that you are doing so well in not thinking about it) you will suddenly notice it entered as a harmless thought about something totally unrelated, and before you know it you are thinking about the problem you were facing. However, the more often you do this when times are tough, the more conscious you become. That's the process. That's the way to Self-Realisation or Enlightenment: Simply feeling the emotion while holding the imagination still, and not getting lost in either.

So, is it okay to think happy thoughts? Short answer: NO! When you are Enlightened and can think about anything without being moved emotionally and removed from being, then maybe. But thinking feeds the emotional mind, whether good thinking or bad, and both take you away from the knowledge of being complete now. The more you think nice thoughts when you are happy and all's okay, the harder you will find it to halt the momentum when something happens to bring up an unhappy thought.

By way of summary, the way is to begin to slow the mind when it tries to think, by holding on to your awareness that you exist, in good times and bad, thus dissolving the emotion that is driving it which in turn becomes weaker, so has less power to make you think anyway.

Here are a few exercises you can do to assist in regaining some control over your mind and emotions and begin to realise, or release, your power behind it.

Other Exercises

1) Break any habits. If there is anything you do purely out of habit, stop. Do the opposite or something totally different. The purpose of this is to break the momentum, making you more conscious. The action itself is not the point and there is no judgement here. It's all about being conscious and not on autopilot all the time.

2) Acknowledge the good that you see in your life and around you. The emotions love negativity and dwell in doom and gloom. That is why the newspapers are full of it. By acknowledging the good you see around you, be it a nice day, a flower, someone's clothes, their hair, anything, even if it is silently to yourself, this again breaks the momentum of the mind and emotions. When you are acknowledging anything, you are more conscious.

3) Be aware of your body. This should perhaps have been at the top and is a very important part of becoming conscious: to be aware of your body and where it is and what it is doing. We spend so much of our lives in emotion and imagination that we have lost touch with the simplicity of just being. The first step to doing this is to be aware of your breathing. This serves to calm the mind, making it easier to hold on to the awareness of the rest of the body.

You cannot be aware of your body all the time, as you can only really focus on one thing at a time. In action you often must have your full attention on what you are doing, or you may make a mistake. Just come back when you can in between the action, be it when seated on a bus, standing in a queue, waiting for someone or something – in fact, whenever you are reminded from within to feel your body and notice where you are. Just be aware 'I am' and hold

15

on to this as long as you are able to. Every time you do so will make it that bit easier the next time you get emotional to hold on to your being and not to lose yourself in the imagination and feelings of the situation.

4) Don't accept the thought! It is very easy when you catch yourself thinking to find the emotion urging you to complete the scenario you were thinking about before stopping. You need to deny it this momentum. Dropping it instantly will make you stronger and make it easier for you to stop when things are difficult. The pang of attachment will pass after only a second or two, but you need to be strong enough to stand it for that short period, despite its claims that it will go on forever if it can't finish the daydream.

5) Don't take on board the emotions of others. You are responsible for your actions and your thoughts and feelings. You are not responsible for the feelings of anyone else. Their feelings are selfish and will control you and manipulate you. Don't accept any of it. By all means be aware of them and understand their vulnerability, but there is a fine line between understanding and being their whipping boy.

6) Don't expect anyone to accept your emotions either. They are yours. Deal with the situation as best you can, but be responsible and deal with your own selfish hurts and pains. Don't blame someone else for what you are holding on to through stubbornness and a sense of superiority and justification for what you think they have done.

7) Don't judge. Everyone is doing their best, even if it's not very good. Even if it means you leave them, do not judge them. You can only be what you are, as anyone can. The less you judge yourself, the less you'll judge others, and vice-versa. Learn and move on. Say sorry if appropriate, but learn and move on.

8) Deny the wants. The mind thinks about what it wants and imagines having something. This is dishonest. In women this may be new clothes, food, holidays – in fact anything to make up for the lack of love she is receiving from her partner and the world around her. In men this is often sex. Man must stop lusting after Woman. Otherwise when he really gets near her physically he finds he can't love her. He

16

has spent so long thinking about being with her that he can't stop thinking when he gets there and is impatient and wanting. Excitement is not love. There is nothing wrong with working for something, or with having something or enjoying it. It is the imagination, with its wanting, that we are watching here.

9) Know that you cannot fail. Life is here for you to learn from. Lessons happen to teach you. If something happens and you get emotional, do not think you have failed. That would be the mind thinking, judging and dwelling: all stuff we are trying not to do. Just know that everything happens for a reason, and that reason is to teach you. You cannot fail. You can only learn.

10) Know that life is perfect. This is your life. It is tailored to you to give you the experiences you need; though not necessarily the ones you want. Trust you will be looked after, even if you don't see how yet. You just need to be open to receive each lesson as it is presented, to learn it as fast as you can and move on. It is by dwelling on situations that we get stuck in them and don't seem to progress. Learn and move on. Hold on to nothing.

11) Nothing is the truth. The only truth really is the space inside you: your 'being' – the stillness or space of no-thing where there is no feeling. That is life, and is as close as you can get to the source of all things. Hold it, feel it, be it as much as you can. When it is a constant state, you will be Enlightened!

Good luck and stick with it. (Though it is happening here whether we are aware of it or not. Everyone gets 'there' in the end.)

I have found, perhaps not surprisingly, that most people don't want to know about how to be Enlightened but how to deal with everyday living; that is, how to deal with the problems we have to face each and every day in our lives. The answer to this question is actually on almost every page in this book, but it seemed time to devote a page to this subject.

Dealing with Problems

A problem is a negative emotional reaction to a situation, real or imagined. The situation itself is not the 'problem'. It is the interpretation as to how it affects 'me' that turns a situation into a problem. The way to deal with a problem is two-fold:

   1) Look logically and practically at the situation while as much as possible keeping the emotions out of it, and see what can be done to address the problem <u>now</u>. However, be aware the problem is actually the emotion, not the external situation, so the aim is really to free oneself of the feeling. The whole world cannot be changed at once, so don't get too involved in trying to change things that cannot, or don't need to be, changed.

   2) Once you have done all you can see that can be done at this time to fix the problem (and be aware that just because there may be nothing more you can do now, things can, and do, change) the next step is to face the emotion which is creating the problem. This is done by holding the knowledge of the situation and not thinking about it (which is going round in circles, imagining). By being aware of the problem, holding it and not wallowing in it, you are denying the emotion the power it needs from the imagination to survive, and it will shrivel and die.

   The feeling as this happens is quite uncomfortable, but the less you feed emotions by thinking, and instead look practically at situations and what can be done and just hold the emotion still, you will find you have fewer and fewer problems.

18

It is vital to understand that no matter how hard you work at facing emotion, if there is action that needs to be taken and you are too scared or perhaps too lazy (or for whatever other reason) to take the action, your mind and emotions will not let you rest. This is not a teaching that allows a person to ignore everything and do nothing. Life must be lived here, and fears must be faced.

Every time a feeling arises that is disturbing, the first thing to do is to not just accept it or ignore it. Your space should be free from problems and worry. Have a look at what is causing the feeling. Is it something that really is 'wrong' and can and should be changed, or is it an innocent thing which is reminding you about a past experience; or perhaps even a combination of the two: that is to say, perhaps this thing does indeed need to be addressed and action taken in the here and now, but it is also very similar to an earlier situation which caused similar feelings. If it is the latter, if you can do this and hold the knowledge of the situation without imaginings, you are actually facing and dissolving both emotional attachments at once: the present pain and the past. As the situations are so similar, the emotion is the same. By facing one here and now, the past emotion which came up is also being faced, acknowledged and dissolved; thus you are becoming free of the past hurts.

As each situation is faced, the person becomes lighter, their life easier and they find they have fewer and fewer problems. Whatever the cause, the above directions need to be followed in every case in order to become free of problems.

Enlightenment is to have no problems, as everything is faced as it occurs with no holding on. My own space of being and peace within is precious, and if anything is disturbing this I cannot accept it; no matter how frightening the action may be that I know I must take to be free of it.

So to deal with a problem (and don't try to do two different problems at once, it doesn't work), the procedure is simply to look practically at what can be done to change it. Take the action that is seen and needs to be taken, and then dissolve the remaining emotion by feeling and holding the knowledge of it, denying the mind from imagining and reliving it. Good luck. It does get easier.

19

☯ 🕉 ✡ ☸ ☪ ✝

Here I am focusing not on *how* to do it, but on what is required *to* do it. That is, what sort of attitude or state of mind is needed to actually reach the state of Enlightenment? I have known people attend a Master's talks year after year, buying all books and tapes and videos that are released, and yet maybe ten or fifteen years later seem to have made little or no progress towards the state they are looking for. Why?

Can Anybody Do This?

I am going to liken it to running a marathon. It may be broadly true to say anybody could do it, given the training, time and motivation to get into shape. That's not to say we would all want to. Those that do train and focus on the goal (of getting to the end as fast as they can) are likely to do well, but they may also possess an innate tendency towards the practice so have an advantage anyway. The others may still reach the finish, but without the motivation, the drive or natural ability so they take much longer to reach the end. Many may even walk it. Some wear costumes to make it more entertaining. All will get there, but how and when depends on a number of factors.

Pain and struggle? The spiritual teachings of the East often describe how the way is to withdraw from all the pleasures of this life, to live in caves as hermits or in large monasteries, wearing plain robes, shaving heads and spending hours in meditation and prayer. Some deny themselves hot baths or showers and other such simple pleasures. Some even whip themselves and many practise some sort of physical pain or endurance in the endeavour to reach Enlightenment.

Here in the West we are very reluctant to give up anything. We read great books about the Eastern monks and Spiritual Masters, only to carry on our own way in the belief that the experience is only really available to those who lived in those times and places, and who are moved to put themselves through such hardship; but it's not for us.

Again, there is a middle way: We have to live here; to eat, sleep, walk, talk and interact with the environment here. That is not the problem. If you enjoy something, why not do it? Doing or not doing something will not make you Enlightened; so what will?

The state or experience is a state of mind, not of body. It is not about *what* you do, but *why* you do it, how you feel about it and, more importantly, how you would feel if you couldn't do it. The state is to want nothing beyond what is here now; to enjoy whatever I am doing now and yet know it will not last. Then, when the experience ends, it is being able to accept and move on with no thought of holding on to what has gone, or wanting what is not.

To achieve this may involve the practice of not doing things, solely because I know I am attached to doing them. If I know (if I am truly honest with myself) that if something was to be taken from me (which anything and everything can be at any moment) it would upset me, I may purposely not allow myself to do it through choice. I will deny myself and break my attachment before the thing is taken from me. Later I may return to it, but in the knowledge that, although I enjoy it, if I were to lose it, it would not be the end of the world, of my world. I am not necessarily talking of self-denial here, but we can see the similarity. We are seeing if we can have a break from the habit or continuation and break the attachment in one's own way in one's own time, instead of waiting for life to take it away from you. However, all attachments will be broken at some time, so you don't really need to do anything at all.

The only thing preventing you from experiencing the one being, from being 'Enlightened', is the emotion within you controlling you and acting through you. You need to deny this what it wants wherever and whenever you see it, to take its energy and reclaim yours. It is feeding off you after all. That is why you can feel exhausted after an emotional time.

However, the emotion wants you to feel it. Whether it is as excitement, regret, anger, jealousy, fear, happiness or unhappiness, to name a few, all these are emotional feelings that do not last. They

21

take your energy and exert their own power over you. It is as if you have two personalities: the one where you are in a good mood and the one where you are in a bad mood. However, there is a third state not often appreciated where you are simply aware and enjoying being where you are as a constant state, with little or no feeling in it. You just need to face and get through the emotion to find this state for any length of time.

So, in answer to the initial question, yes, anybody in theory could be Enlightened. (Though it seems it does require the reflective ability of our human brain. It could be said animals are already Enlightened in the sense of being alert and conscious all the time, but as they are not reflective but are instinctive, they don't know it.)

What is required is the drive to spot and to break any and all emotional attachments as they are shown, but not necessarily to endure physical hardships and forced emotional trauma or have cold showers. Be careful of the emotional attachment to 'progressing' sending you off on a tangent, where you put yourself in unnecessarily difficult situations for long periods of time while telling yourself you are being more 'spiritual' because you are enduring these. This can actually feed the emotion as it inflates with the pride of its apparent achievements.

Anything that induces an emotional feeling needs to be viewed with suspicion and watched very carefully, and if seen as an attachment to an experience or object, steps should be taken to face and dissolve this. It may be difficult to see but if this starts to become your life, you will begin to notice that things seem to be taken from you to help you break the attachment so you can progress. Where I am now, life often just shows me the possibility of me losing something to expose the emotion. I accept that I may be about to lose the thing, face and dissolve the emotion, and most times find the thing is not taken anyway. It was to be taken to break the attachment in me, but if I break it first by facing and dissolving the rising emotion, there is no need for me to lose it and I get to keep it. There is indeed one consciousness looking after all your existence, and it starts within you.

☯ ॐ ✡ ☸ ☪ ✝

Looking for a simple, direct route to Enlightenment? Here are my three steps:

Three Steps to Enlightenment

1) Practise being aware of where you are and of what you are feeling.

2) Start now!

3) Keep doing it!

Is that simple enough?

What is likely to happen is you will read the above, and perhaps even understand it, but the truth of it will not penetrate your thinking mind and emotions with its longing to find something.

If you are truly looking to find the truth, to find yourself, to find God within you, then you need look no further than what you are feeling now, at this very moment. Feel it? Do you feel the space inside where you are aware you exist? That's it! That's you before you become anything; before you begin thinking and feeling and become separate. Self-Realisation is realising what you already are. You will never be complete while you look for something else; that's the secret!

23

I call it a secret, not only because the truth of it is beyond the understanding of most people, but because it seems very hard to find someone who is actually Enlightened. Why?

The Secret of Enlightenment

The whole spiritual community, with all its traditions and philosophies, teachings and practices, are all looking for Enlightenment. There are many stories as to what it means to be Enlightened and for many it is the Holy Grail of the spiritual life.

When a person actually attains Enlightenment, truly, they realise it is not what they, or anybody else, thought. It is far simpler, potentially far more frightening, gives far more responsibility than ever imagined and yet, despite this, the experience awards no real answers as to who or what 'I' am. For these reasons the individual is often reluctant to admit to being Enlightened, concerned also by the attitudes of those around who are likely to either disbelieve their claims or set them up as some god to be worshipped. Therefore, if they are moved to pass on the knowledge of the experience to others, the individual may avoid the question of their own level of Self-knowledge and write or teach in the third person. To me this is a shame, as it denies those around from experiencing the full authority of the words and their source, leaving the impression that it could still be some hypothetical reasoning or belief system like all the others. That is to say, this person telling them what Enlightenment is could be wrong, if they aren't actually Enlightened. The situation is made more confusing by spiritual teachers still 'on the path' who don't really want to admit to not being Enlightened, so also avoid the question while implying they are.

You can see from this that if both Enlightened and un-Enlightened teachers avoid the question as to whether they are or are not Enlightened, it makes it increasingly difficult to know what Enlightenment really is. So the only ones left to 'follow' are those

24

people who do openly declare it. This can open the way for two types. The first could be seen as 'tyrants', such as those who are truly Enlightened but claim to be God and encourage people to worship them (the Enlightened man or woman). To me a true teacher should be teaching those around to realise the truth within themselves, so telling them to worship the teacher is confusing them, not teaching them. The second type are those that aren't actually Enlightened at all but claim they are, thus confusing people as much as the true Masters who are just setting themselves up as something special, as they may actually give misinformation, whether intentional or not.

Since setting up the website on Enlightenment I have spent some time on the internet and have been amazed at how many websites there are that look at this subject. Many are discussing possible meanings of the word, while others teach their view as to what it is. Despite all this, it seems hard to find one where the individual actually states they are Enlightened (and can demonstrate it). Many imply it, but few state it. I have been to a couple of talks by a spiritual teacher of many years who teaches the subject of Enlightenment and yet seems to avoid the subject as to whether or not he is Enlightened. He isn't (to me), and to my knowledge he doesn't claim to be, but the implication does seem to be there.

Then I have more recently met a lovely guy who is Enlightened, has been for over fifteen years, and has even written books on the subject. However, he is careful not to state that he is Enlightened due to all the ideas as to what it is (which is why he has to write the books in the first place; because no one knows what it is).

You may have noticed that I state that I am Enlightened. I do this so you have a point of reference. If there is another Enlightenment then I too would like to know about it; but I know of no other besides a deepening of the one I have. My aim is to make the state accessible to us 'normal folk': to those of us who don't speak Sanskrit, who don't live in monasteries or wear robes, and who have to drive to work each day to pay the bills. My words are as straight and as simple as I can make them. A person still has to be ready to hear them, but at least when you are ready you don't have to go far or study hard to understand. The state of Enlightenment is simply what you are behind your thoughts, beliefs and feelings. Stay with it. 'It' is your true nature; the space you feel now, where you are aware that you exist, where you are aware that 'I am'. This is the secret.

There are many teachers and teachings of Enlightenment. Most agree generally on what Enlightenment is.

However, it seems as well as there being many different methods and practices and techniques to assist on the path, some even teach...

You Are Already Enlightened!

Well, that's what they say. Perhaps you have heard it. 'You are already Enlightened; there is nothing you can do or need to do because you are already there.'

Well now that's cleared up, we can all go home (metaphorically speaking). So what now? If the above is true why are you still reading this...or indeed any of the stuff on Enlightenment? (I am assuming you do not think you are Enlightened.)

If you are Enlightened, according to all the definitions I have come across (said in various ways), you would know that the being you are is creating all that is, that you are not separate; indeed you are in the uninterrupted experience of being the space or intelligence before anything exists. You are the infinite and the timeless without beginning or end...are you? If you are not, then perhaps the above statements are incorrect! Perhaps you are not already there!?

When we look at teachers who say the above phrase, we find they even describe a time in their lives, often involving many years of searching and practices, when they would not have claimed to be Enlightened. So why do they now say they have always been Enlightened?

What has happened is they have realised what they are and what they have always been behind what they thought they were...or perhaps more accurately have realised what they are not. The experience is just 'I am this' or 'I am nothing' or similar descriptions, '...and yet I am complete'. It is true in all definitions that the experience is of 'Self-realisation', so you are realising your self as it

27

already is, but I would suggest, therefore, that by definition until you are 'Self-realised' – that is, you have made real in your experience your 'true' self – you are not Enlightened. That is not to say it cannot occur at any moment, but until it happens, it hasn't.

So, if you want to hold on to the belief that you are already Enlightened etc, that's okay; but I don't think it helps you very much. When you have problems in your life – when you lose people you love, either through death or because they leave you; when life does not seem to go your way and is really tough; when you face death and feel the fear, or even long for death to put an end to your own suffering; when you are having arguments and fights with strangers as well as with those you are supposed to love; when you long to be shown some reason or truth behind what is here, or you pray desperately for an end to the turmoil and emotional pain – just remember 'You are already Enlightened!', so what's the problem? The problem is, of course, that Enlightenment is a realisation, not a statement. Stating it does not make it so.

I'm being a little facetious here, but this is my own name given to the latest craze or fashion in spiritual 'groups', clubs or teachings. This club costs nothing to join and requires only that you are able to churn out by rote over and over a certain idea, no matter what is asked of you. So, what is the NHC?

Are You a Member of the NHC?

The NHC stands for the 'Nobody Here Club'. Have you heard this one? 'There is nobody here to be or not be Enlightened, and this is nothing happening to nobody!'

This catchy little phrase is now being repeated time after time in some quarters by people who have no personal experience of the truth of it at all. It is a great way to seem like you know what you are talking about, while avoiding having to do anything or know anything; or even having to take any responsibility at all for anything you think, say or do. Great, isn't it? You can abuse people, you can lie and cheat, you can do anything you like and should you be questioned you can repeat, 'There is nobody here to do anything and there is nobody there to know it anyway!'

To an Enlightened person it is true that he or she has realised the point of being before anything exists, in the experience and the knowledge that 'I' only exist in this dream and therefore have no reality; and as there is no knowledge of anything beyond this dream, I can say 'this dream is being had by no one'. Hence we have the expression, 'This is nothing happening to no one!' Okay. I understand.

While I agree up to a point, I was asked this question the other week: 'Nick, to you, is there anyone here?' I had a look at what was being felt here, within this body, and had to reply, 'There is something here to know the question is being asked and to look inside to see this. Therefore I must say, yes, there is something here because whatever I am, I am here!'

It is unfortunate that this 'there's nobody here' idea is so easy to learn and churn out, because it can be difficult to tell who has any real self-knowledge and who is acting as a human tape-recorder; that is, until you have heard it a few times.

You are likely to come across these types, particularly if you visit forums, and no matter how hard you try to interact with them, there is often nothing you can do or say to interrupt their rhythm. Whichever one of their members you come across, and their numbers are growing fast, you will recognise the droning. It is a little like invasion of the body-snatchers and you cannot talk to some of them in any real way, even to ask whether they really know it or have just read it, as it is likely to produce the answer 'There is nobody to know or do anything!'.

I do wonder, though, if those saying this would hold fast to it were they to lose someone they truly love; perhaps if they had to watch as a loved one suffered or died in an accident? I wonder if reminding them at that time 'It's okay; there is nobody to die and there is nobody to miss them' would be welcomed?

Do what you will. It is true that life will happen as it does, but on this level you do have influence. You know you are here, because you can feel it now (can't you?). Whether the person next to you is here in the same way as you are is another matter entirely, as you can't feel what they are feeling; but as you are not trying to realise the truth within them it doesn't matter. You can only realise anything within you. Keep going, although you can do nothing else. 'I' am here (the stillness where you are aware that you exist). Do you feel it?

We have heard Enlightened Masters declaring that they have finished. That Enlightenment is the end.

If that were true, they would no longer have need of a body and would not be here. The truth is actually far scarier for those striving to reach this state: to be told that Enlightenment is not the end at all, but is actually just a step in the process.

After Enlightenment, What Now?

Enlightenment is simply having dissolved enough emotion, enough past, to be in touch with the being behind the forms, and having the knowledge of why things happen and what to do about them.

It, in itself, is not the end, though it may be called 'the beginning of the end'; or even just 'a new beginning', as the end is uncertain.

What happens in me now is, as a situation occurs that causes some feeling, I see very quickly it has happened to expose this bit of emotion not yet faced, perhaps even before the feeling rises, and I am able to face it and dissolve it quickly. Therefore the need for existence continues to be dissolved with each new experience and the experience becomes finer. When enough emotion has been dissolved, there will be no more need for existence, no more need for things to appear separate, and the projection will end.

So what is after death? Tricky question: If a person dies before they are Enlightened and before they have dissolved the need for existence, then I would say *the* being (their own being) creates another body to continue creating or dissolving emotion (depending on whether it is on the way out or the way back to its being). However, if the person has dissolved the need for existence and the existence evaporates for them, then I am stuck as to exactly what happens next. I could say the being returns to its state of not being as all the need for existence will have been satisfied, but the truth is that there is no knowledge beyond this experience here and now. It may be that there isn't any knowledge of the next from this side.

31

To explain this further, this existence has been likened to a dream and being Enlightened is like knowing you are dreaming. When asleep at night, no matter how aware you are that you are dreaming, you still have no awareness of the bed your body is lying in or the colour of your bedroom etc. The point here is again that there really are no answers beyond the knowledge that my being, whatever it is, is creating this. I can know I am dreaming everything I experience and this is all with the one, which is my own intelligence (how could it not be mine if there is only one?). However, everything that is realised is realised within the dream. That is to say, even 'the truth', as it is experienced here, is still only dreamt. I can say I know all this, but I also know I am dreaming, and if I am dreaming then I am only dreaming that I know I am dreaming. Get it?

The dream of life

In Nov '94, I sent a letter to Barry Long describing an insight I had been given, that this is like a dream. He replied and confirmed it.

On receiving his letter I saw no point in continuing with all this, if it's only a dream. I spent three days at home in my dressing gown not bothering to get dressed, sitting and just staring at the four walls almost in a state of shock from the feeling of entrapment, isolation and hopelessness of the situation. On the third day, still struggling to cope with the feelings inside, the following phrase came to me, as if from the depths of my being, to inform me, real or not, this has to be done. I got up and went to work.

'A dream it may be,

But the dream goes on.'

By Nick Roach, Nov '94

32

The state of Enlightenment is commonly accepted as the ultimate goal of life, whether through conscious searching or just unconscious living over time. It is indeed very rare to find a person who has reached this apparently elusive experience. However, there is another half of Enlightenment which is even less publicised.

The Other Half of Enlightenment

We have seen that Enlightenment is the experience, as a constant state, of being the intelligence behind all that is, with the knowledge that even the sense of 'I' is part of this creation which will not last, and yet 'I' have no end. Most if not all of the very few Enlightened individuals we know about describe this as the ultimate experience. What else could there be but to realise, as a constant experience, that one's own consciousness is creating all existence, also known as 'God Realisation'?

Many of these individuals are celibate and also describe how hard it is to remain so, often needing to withdraw from society and temptation. Many others are blatantly promiscuous and even abuse their position as a spiritual teacher and take advantage of their students, and then others claim to be celibate but are later found not to be. Why? Why is this pull to be with woman (if you are a man) so hard to resist? There are, of course, evolutionary explanations such as the genetic need to reproduce, but there is another less known reason, even to the Enlightened few...

The realisation of love

What does this mean? On the page 'What is love?' we will look at how an Enlightened individual is said to be in a state of love all the time as everything is experienced as his/her own reflection, but that is not the same as realising love. The truth of existence is realised as 'I am this' and in this 'I' am complete and whole; but then the dream must still be lived. What more can one do? Well, one can make love

33

real here in the world, and not just as an internal personal knowledge that all is one and where love here in existence doesn't seem to matter.

(Talking to man here) there is a strong attraction to woman (the essence within all women) as we know, but we also know relationships can be so difficult. It is believed by many in spiritual teachings that relationships result in man losing his power in various ways, and therefore abstinence is recommended. Even if it is not true about the life-force being lost through ejaculation, it is known that the stress of trying to love and live with a woman who has moods and emotional ups and downs is a test to any man's Enlightenment, and it is probably easier to stay out of it altogether. But I will ask, why does she have the emotional ups and downs? If the man is truly Enlightened and has realised this existence is his own reflection, and it is said woman is man's other half (as he is hers), how come his own partner can be so emotional and unhappy at times? The answer is he has not realised the other half of Enlightenment, the half that brings the state of union into existence, into his other half in form, which as we know is woman.

This is man's task: to love the woman enough so that (as long as she is willing) he takes the emotion out of her (or helps her in dissolving her own emotion) and she realises her true state is love. It always has been, behind the emotional covering which had developed during the years of not being loved. As he loves her in consciousness and acknowledges her more, so she opens up inside and becomes the embodiment of the love he yearns for. But now it does not come and go according to what mood she is in; it is constant. She is indeed his love in form, as he is hers; thus together they become the reality behind the story of Adam and Eve: the original man and woman, unburdened and free from worries and stress, enjoying being together in love and constant pleasure and appreciation, in their Garden of Eden.

More can be read about this in 'The Garden of Eden' in the 'Essays and Insights' section.

I have heard and read the word 'Liberation' over the years in association with Enlightenment, and had accepted it as just that: another name for Enlightenment. However, this has turned out not to be the case. Liberation comes later, after Enlightenment.

Liberation

I have also read of Masters saying that the state of Enlightenment is to be 'Ego-less'. By that it is meant to have no sense of 'me' (as I understand it). This was strange to me as it is not in my experience, and I wondered what these Masters were referring to. I now am being shown that, as Enlightenment deepens, a new state called Liberation enters the experience.

It is the sense of 'me' that is the back-bone of all fears and worries. Enlightenment in the first instance is to see and experience things as they are. It is to know and feel that the environment is the reflection of one's own nature; so 'my' world is 'me', or it is my self in form. I continue to live here, amongst the forms and images that I am creating, and I dissolve more of my self as experiences pass. However, I am still aware that there is a 'me' amongst these surroundings.

Liberation is a new state that occurs some time later. I am being given the knowledge of it, but it has not occurred here yet at the time of writing this. It is the Liberation where the individual is said to be truly free.

I will liken it to the comparison between a dream and a movie. Enlightenment is like dreaming, but being awake in the dream to be totally aware that 'I' am dreaming, and that it still must be lived. 'I' am living it. Liberation is more like watching a movie and 'I' am outside, watching the actors on screen. Even if it is filmed in the first person with the viewer as the character in the film, it is still not me. I am outside watching, unaffected by the goings on amongst the images. In the experience of it here, I see arms and legs operating, which

35

indeed could be said to be mine, but 'I' am not doing it. It is all being done for me. I make no decisions, and have no choices. I have nothing to do and nowhere to go, beyond what is seen now.

Enlightenment has the awareness that this is only a dream, like a movie, and I am acting a part. Nothing ever really happens here and it is all my own creation anyway; but it is still 'me' doing everything, and indeed being everything. Liberation takes 'me' out of it totally and there is only the movie or what is.

It may be asked, who is watching the movie then? And reasonably it must be said: 'I' am. But that is not the experience. The movie with its images gives the illusion that 'I' must be here, which is what caused everything else to follow from there; but there is no 'me' in Liberation. There are only the images.

So what is creating the images? Remove them and what is left? As usual, here we run out of answers. It's a little like a person who is an authority in a certain religion still having no knowledge of the source or substance of the God upon which his whole religion is based. Or, in a more worldly example, like a computer technician having no knowledge of the source of electricity but still being able to work wonders, as he understands and accepts it and its behaviour. Take away the images and we have deep, dreamless sleep. That is as near to an answer as I can give.

It is strange, though, because no matter how far back we question, we will always look for a beginning. In essence any 'beginning' must be a point before anything exists, and that is what we are looking at here. But then we have the question, how did 'something', whatever it is, occur from nothing? It seems this is a never-ending question here. Thankfully the state of Enlightenment awards an acceptance of what is so, although 'I' am aware of the lack of answers, I am not disturbed by this. I just am (until I am not).

☯ ॐ ✡ ☸ ☪ ✝

There is still a lot of mystery about what Enlightenment really is and therefore who is Enlightened and who isn't.

This page has been written following my talking with and reading about a number of individuals claiming to be Enlightened, having had recent experiences of 'love' and 'oneness'.

Are You Enlightened?

I have worked hard, and continue to do so, to teach people that Enlightenment is not reserved for 'monks or hermits in caves'. I started my spiritual journey reading Patanjali's Yoga Aphorisms, about ancient Yogis who could levitate and appear and disappear at will. This was therefore my preconception about Enlightenment and I had to let go of these ideas. Certain powers may indeed occur, as anything is theoretically possible in consciousness, but they are not the point and are not necessary to be Enlightened; and even if they were present this still would not prove Enlightenment.

The view still exists amongst some traditions and philosophies that Enlightenment – also known as 'God Realisation' and 'Self-realisation' – turns a person into a god who can indeed move mountains.

However, there is a new concern: that as the state is so little understood, it opens the way for anyone with a candle and a yoga mat to claim to be Enlightened. Or even if they have had a profound insight or experience into the state, again it seems increasingly common for those concerned to announce they are now Enlightened, in their innocence not realising that there are numerous insights, experiences and realisations *en route* to Enlightenment, each one giving the impression of being there.

True Enlightenment is beyond the experiences that come and go. It is a constant state of pure being, where only 'now' exists. I do not say I was Enlightened last week, last month, last year or ten years ago. I am Enlightened NOW. I am in the place as a conscious experience where there is no time. There is only being.

I have no problems, no worries, and my life is a constant pleasure, each and every moment. I am 'God-Realised', not as something that happened or happens occasionally. It is here now.

So the truth, as is so often the case, is neither of these two extremes. It is neither having super-human powers, nor is it as common as having an interest in spiritual matters, or even having an amazing experience of love for everyone. Enlightenment could be said to be the highest point of evolution here (taking the end of the dream to be the ultimate) and from then the state deepens. Most people have to work very hard for years, dissolving emotion and facing anything that arises, to reach this state. Some do get it as a flash, but often this seems to pass, leaving the person talking about it for the rest of their life, trying to get it back.

So, know it is possible to be Enlightened in this lifetime. Know it is your true nature and it is not really a secret which is for the chosen few. But know too that it is usually the end of a very long journey of inner work and a flash of experience or insight in one's early twenties (or whatever age) does not qualify the person to claim to be Enlightened. Doing so takes away from the truly Enlightened who can talk from direct experience of living it now and dilutes the true meaning of the word, serving to further confuse genuine seekers who see apparently Enlightened people popping up everywhere. Enjoy the experiences that are given to you. Live them. But know that all experiences are towards Enlightenment. You are not there yet.

On a slightly different note, it is common for men to try to 'be something' with their arrogance and testosterone driving them. Watch out for this. This is the bit of you that is not Enlightened. You are not special, however Enlightened you may or may not be. You are not here to save the world and you are not here to be important, all of which is an attempt to further inflate the arrogant self-importance. There is only the state of being which you are returning to by dissolving your self. But dissolve it you will. Keep going.

I have received a number of emails from people claiming they are Enlightened. They have truly had great insights and experiences of truth and being. They believe they have experienced God, that they have arrived, have nowhere else to go and that their life is complete.

Seeing the openness in one and his wish to really know the truth, after a few emails had passed between us I sent an email containing a very deep question to test the extent of his insight.

This page contains my email as I wrote it, and the two emails that followed (his name has been changed).

Do You Still Think You're Enlightened?

Hi, Simon.

Okay, here's a question for you...There have been Enlightened persons in the past who have stated they are not going to teach anyone, because there is no one here to teach.

When I first was given insight into the same knowledge, I cried (through the fear of being alone). The next time it occurred, a few years later, it became a constant knowledge to be accessible at any moment, after which I didn't bother to get dressed for three days. I gave up, as I saw that nobody and nothing else was real but me, and that this is/was my dream to live, alone.

This is a major part of Enlightenment: to not only know there is nobody else here and you are creating all your family and friends in this dream world, but ultimately the experience is that when you interact with another person, you are aware you are really only talking to an image in your own dream. (This experience may come many years after the knowledge and it may be many years later still that it becomes a constant experience.)

So the question is, Simon, what do you think of the above? (I don't usually spell it out quite that bluntly, as the knowledge can be terrifying, even for people who are ready for it, but you have had some insight so I felt okay to test it. I hope you don't mind.)

Simon replied the next day...

Hello again, Nick.

Well, this question is very interesting and throws me into a logical quandary. I'll admit that I do not walk around thinking that everyone is a figment of my imagination or dream world.

I do agree that life is a dream to the extent that we can control how we feel, regardless of the situation, but regardless of how I look or feel towards something, I would still say that it is there. I would not say that I have created my friends and family, because I can see the pain they are in and know that they need help.

Why are there websites and books, etc and people that say they are Enlightened, like yourself, if they are all part of my dream? You are trying to help people. What is the point if there is no one to help? Then you would be part of my dream and not even exist. So am I just writing a letter to myself then?

Well, this has been an interesting question to deal with. If I failed and am not Enlightened, so be it, but I don't know what I am then, 'cause I'm pretty damn happy and life doesn't bother me. I didn't even know what the concept of Enlightenment was until after I changed my mind and perception of reality. Then I looked it up and decided that is what I had achieved because I have control over my consciousness.

Hope to hear what you think of all this, or if you think I still have some looking to do.

Simon

I replied again...

Hi, Simon.

All's well. You haven't failed. There is no failure. You have had amazing experiences which now must be lived. You have read what I wrote and it was necessary for you to do so. It will work in you now and some time in the not too distant future you will indeed receive glimpses of the knowledge we are speaking of. Any fear that comes up is only the emotion not yet faced. It will pass. There is no more 'looking to do', as you have found it. You just can't have it all at

40

once. There is indeed more living to do, but this is the same for anyone still here.

You also asked about teachers and why they teach if they have realised there is no one else here? Well, first I suggest a proportion of them probably don't have this level of self-knowledge and therefore really think they are doing something here (saving the world, or whatever).

As for those that do and still teach, like myself, one must do something. I still have existence here. I still must get up in the morning, go to the bathroom, have breakfast, go to work etc. While I am here I may as well see if I can teach fellow beings (dreamt or otherwise) to realise the truth, and the more people that feel it, the greater reflection of my own being I get back. I do avoid being around emotional, unhappy people and I find it a pleasure being around people who take responsibility for their own feelings, so in teaching others I am also improving my own environment. I either do this or withdraw totally from the world and its aggressive sexuality. I have chosen to stay and continue to take part.

'Then you would be part of my dream and not even exist. So am I just writing a letter to myself then?' Yes, that is the truth. However, there is an old saying: 'We are all created equal.' You (God) has created this dream, but in doing so has created it so that all the other people/images are also able to 'apparently' realise they are God. This means there is no point running round claiming to be God, because either people would say you are mad, or you may come across another Enlightened person who claims they are God. And in truth, you (Simon) are not God. Simon is the separation from God which allows God to experience being. When Simon has dissolved enough of his emotional self, the need for existence in any form will have been satisfied. The dream will end and there will again be only God.

I explain this more on the page 'Does the Devil Exist, and If So Who Is He?', as well on the page 'The Tree of Life'.

Thanks, Simon. Keep well and keep going.

Nick Roach

Insights

Not directly related to Enlightenment itself, here I look at various subjects, some in answer to common spiritual questions and others that have just came up in conversation. Either way, they are a good example of how the experience can affect one's perspective and questions of many years are no longer questions: the answers instead become almost self-explanatory when it is all put together.

You have no doubt asked this question at some time...perhaps you are still asking it. There are many theories and practices looking at who or what you are and how you go about 'finding yourself', so let's have a look at this and see if we can't answer the question here and now:

Who Am I?

You may have heard it said, and perhaps you accept the idea, that there is one being here: one God or consciousness, intelligence, mind or awareness, to give it a few labels. Well, if there is one God or intelligence here creating all of this, and you are here asking 'Who am I?', how many options are there?!

Can you see how simple it is? I'll ask you that again: If there really is one God here (creating everything each and every moment) and you are here, where is this God or great consciousness? It's obvious, isn't it? Well, it should be, but it is very difficult for the mind to grasp this, not because there is anything wrong but because it's a little like looking directly into the sun. It is not usually done safely.

Okay, the space you feel inside when you are aware of where you are and of what you are feeling, is GOD! How could it be anything else? We have, after all, agreed there is nothing else here, so anything here must be it! And since you are here (check again), you must be it.

But that's too simple, too direct. If we are able to accept there is one being or God here creating everything, then 'we' (you) are likely to convince yourself, very quickly, 'Yes, there is one being, but I am only a *part* of it!' I will ask you then, where did this 'part' come from? It would also imply there are other parts, thus actually more than one, when we have already accepted there is only one, AND YOU ARE IT!!!

You are unlikely to know this yet, which is how it should be until it's time to see past it, but to save you spending any more time

45

searching for your 'self', let's deal with it here so you will always know where your 'self' is...You are it!!! Okay, got that? No? Still too simple?

Okay, the space you are feeling inside, the space behind any disturbance that may be within you: that space is you! Where did you think you were? What did you think you were?

The trouble is, as far as experiencing it goes, because you are already it, you are already it! Have you got it? That means there is nothing to feel because you are already there! So trying to find Enlightenment or Self-Realisation in the form of some great experience is not going to happen. And if you have had great experiences and you are trying to get them back, then you are not going to find your 'self' until you stop looking for something outside yourself. The thing that's doing the looking is it! Simple, isn't it!?

So, what can you do? Just carry on with your life, doing whatever you do, but be aware as often as you can of where you are and of what you are feeling. The more you do this, the more you become the 'space' that's doing the 'looking': that is, the more you realise your 'self'.

So, what do you find when you realise your 'self'? Well, if you were looking for some flashing lights, if you were looking for all the answers and the ability to walk through walls, you are likely to be disappointed, because all you realise is the space you have always been, and that it is all there is!

Yes, you read that right. You realise the space within you, the space you have always been, is all that is real and everything comes out of that. In short, you realise that space is God, which is why this has also been called 'God-Realisation'. But before you get any ideas of grandeur, you have realised the space is God, but also that nothing is real as it all comes out of that space. That means even your own body is not real here, nor is anything else you experience. Suddenly you are alone within your own dream, aware that anyone you talk to is within your own mind, your own creation. Your life really is whatever you make it because it is your own emotional state determining what happens to you. This includes all your experience, whether it is who dies or leaves you, who you meet, what you win or

46

lose, when you achieve and when you fail. This is your life and yours alone. Your life couldn't be anyone else's. There is only one being here and you have seen you are that!

So, having established 'Who I am' (meaning you), let's ask 'What am I?'.

Here we run out of answers. Even if you are truly Self-Realised or Enlightened, there are still no answers. The self-knowledge is only realising what you already are, so nothing new there. And as you realise your own being is creating everything that you experience, there is still no knowledge as to who or what 'this' is, other than 'I am it!' (you). So you could say 'I am God' or 'I am this!', but you still don't know what you am...just 'I am this!'.

On the other hand, if you don't accept there is only one being here, of course all the other stuff still applies. 'You' are still the space inside where you feel aware. You still don't need to look any further to find yourself and you will still become more aware of it the more you practise being aware of it. In the end the knowledge will still be 'I am this' and you still won't know what 'this' is. And since you will only be able to realise your own being, in your own experience there will still be only one being here, and you find 'you' are it. You just don't perhaps yet accept that there are no others here, but that's okay. Why should you? This is your own dream to enjoy being separate with these others. Don't let me spoil it for you.

Whatever you are doing is what you should be doing, but that doesn't mean you have to keep doing it. Be as aware as you can, as often as you can, of where you are and of what you are feeling. If you do have a 'purpose' here, that is it; but it is happening during your life here anyway whatever you do, so there is no need to rush to achieve it.

The story of Genesis is accepted by most as being just a story. Here I will attempt to put meaning to the story of Adam and Eve in the Garden of Eden, as I see it.

The Garden of Eden

The story here begins with Adam already having been created in form, apparently separate from God. He had no past, no worries and no problems; he was just enjoying the other forms around in the garden God had created. After a time of interacting with the forms and becoming increasingly absorbed and lost in them, God (the one consciousness creating Adam and all forms) saw there was a need for Adam to have a partner similar to himself. As I see it, this new form was to be God in another body which would symbolise the oneness that Adam had left behind by being created. Until any of this had happened there was no Adam and no creation. Adam was the tool through which God could enjoy all else, as a separate form amongst other forms, while still being in touch with his source within, with the knowledge that it was his own being/God within him creating it all.

So Eve was created, similar to Adam but softer, representing the union that Adam could feel within himself. Inside he still knew there was one creator, one God, and he was in touch with this, but outside he was separate. He had so far enjoyed the experience of putting forms such as foods and liquids into his body, giving a sense of completeness for a while, but this new form was different. Eve offered the opportunity for him to not only share the experiences of the various forms with another, but actually share the experience of being one with another in form. Their physical bodies would join and the psyche would again become one, while still being conscious in creation. Within they were each complete in a feeling of peace and wholeness as individuals, and they were together outside in their forms. This enabled them both to unite as one with the power within

48

and without, joining consciously in the making of physical love, bringing them full circle, back to the beginning of the conscious stillness within where it all began.

Then something changed. Life had been blissful, easy and trouble free, until the need for still more experience raised its head again.

The story we know describes the serpent persuading Eve to eat of the Tree of Knowledge and how she persuaded Adam to do so; thus they were cast out of the garden of paradise to struggle and suffer. The story describes how God had noticed Adam had become self-conscious and embarrassed of being naked in front of God as he walked in the garden. To me this is the story of identification with the body and beginning to think and want more than what is here now. Thinking is the process of imagination that removes us from the simplicity of what is now, from the knowledge that all is well here in the Enlightened state of union, and dumps us in our personal, selfish world of emotional problems.

The serpent is often used to symbolise sex, and it could indeed be said that possibly Adam had begun to imagine having sex with Eve in the sense of looking forward to being with her, instead of consciously loving her in the moment, thus leaving the conscious feeling of being complete within. The walls of Eden crumbled as he stepped out of the conscious union with God and Eve and into his cold, lonely world of separation, pain and struggle. From this day forward he and Eve would be bound together in the separation of existence, always longing to be united but doomed to hurt and accuse and blame each other in their selfishness, until again they learned to love and be one, both within and without.

This is a nice story and is the truth to me. The Enlightened man has awakened in the dream of forms to realise that he and God are one; indeed Adam only exists in the forms. However, if he wishes to truly find paradise here, he must find Eve. Eve is the truth in every woman, covered over by past and unconscious love (and unconscious love-making). She has lost her softness and sense of peaceful knowing, to become instead more like man as his lack of love for her leaves her struggling, wanting and trying, and even she

49

does not know how to find the way out. It is now man's task to love his Eve so she can again become one with him amongst the forms; thus they will be together within and without, united in love.

Is it easy to uncover Eve, the original love in woman? Of course it isn't. Adam doesn't get away with centuries of selfishness and abuse and taking her for granted that easily. He must love her consciously as the old emotion of all the years comes to the surface to attack and accuse him, to blame and fight to be left alone in its now accustomed world of pain. He must love and stand fast. He is there for love and he will not be truly complete until he and Eve can return home; return to Eden where they live in constant pleasure and love. Here God is the essence and presence in and around them both, and all is provided each and every moment for their enjoyment, as they continue their journey back to the beginning, back to God.

When asked the question 'Does God exist?', if you accept that Enlightenment is also God Realisation and that there are people who have indeed reached this state of being, then it would seem reasonable to reply: 'Yes, God does exist. Otherwise you could not be God Realised!'

Does God Exist?

However, we use the word or name 'God' to label an intelligence creating this existence. Therefore it would be more accurate to say God does NOT *exist*. If this thing called God is indeed an intelligence creating all existence, then God is not in existence but existence is in God.

This may seem like playing with words, and when the question is asked the questioner is often really asking: 'Is there an intelligence behind this existence, creating it each moment, in the way that we understand the word "God" to represent?' This is a long-winded way to ask it and the answer would be 'Yes'.

It is important to make the above distinction, though, because of what Enlightenment is. This is because Enlightenment is not found here in existence. It is not achieved through any belief or scientific research, or philosophy, or image, or questioning process. Enlightenment, in the sense of God-Realisation (and I say this is what Enlightenment is when truly realised), is the stilling or slowing of the questioning personal mind enough to experience the one being, or intelligence, creating everything, and to know this as one's own being. And furthermore, it is not to have it as a brief experience or even one that comes and goes, but as a constant state of awareness: 'I am this.'

Taking the question further: Who or what is God? And who or what am 'I' to be aware of 'this'?

'God', we have said, is one name we give to whatever the intelligence is (and we only use the word 'intelligence' through lack of

51

any other knowledge) that creates one's environment, and it is experienced here as the point before anything is created as a feeling of nothing, or stillness, or peace within one's own being. With the experience of consciously becoming this space comes a clearer knowledge of life here and how things work, but the experience itself is of just being here, now, aware.

So, to answer the question 'What or who am I, and who is experiencing this?', 'I' (you) must be a part of this intelligence to be here within its creation and in order to experience the stillness and the knowledge as I become more at one with it. So I see, frightening though it is, I must be it. I, whatever 'I' am, ultimately am the intelligence creating all of life here; and yet I am separate from it. How come? How can I be creating it all and yet at the same time be separate?

To answer the above, I know all forms are separate here and also that they are all from and within this being I have realised I am. I also know that no form is the truth and no feeling is the truth. I therefore begin to see that I too, this mind and body, are not the truth, thus will also have to end. I see that 'I' am the separation from the intelligence we call 'God', and after struggling for years amongst the images that are created here I have realised I come from God. 'I' can even say I have realised God as my own being (and some who have realised this have even claimed to be God). However, the knowledge is that all must end, as it began. Eventually there will be no sense of 'me'. There will again be just consciousness with nothing to reflect on, so no knowledge of anything at all as there would be nothing to know or be known; and even no one to know it. It is only through being separate from something that it can be experienced, thus your own nature is experienced according to the nature of the separation and your experience here. There must be separation for the impermanence of it to be seen, just as in the ancient teaching 'It is only through ignorance that the truth can be known'.

In the end, existence only exists while it is experienced, whether this is as a sense of 'me', of God or of any object one may mention. When all is again one and the dream ends, there is nothing to experience and no one to experience it. Then there is nothing.

52

One of the insights or experiences often mentioned in spiritual teachings is seeing that 'I' as a separate entity do not exist; that 'I' (you) am only an illusion. This page details one of my early experiences of this nature.

The Disappearing 'I'

I was sitting with some friends/family at a table in a club in Selsey (Sussex, UK) watching and listening to a band on stage.

Suddenly I had the experience that there was no 'me'. There was the room, the tables and chairs, the stage, the band, the noise, all the people around me, but there was no 'me'. I saw that the images in front of me 'over there' were giving the illusion of me being 'over here', and that I existed at all. The fact was, there was no 'me'. I saw that if the shapes were to be taken away, I would cease to be. It was the shapes giving 'me' something to reflect off and providing a sense of being, like sunlight in space going on forever until it meets an object; until then it cannot be seen.

It has been said in other teachings that 'the observer and the observed become one'. The truth in this experience for me was that there was no 'observer', as the illusion of this evaporated, leaving only the observed; but observed by whom, by what?

It is now several years later and I still have the knowledge of this experience. It may be that the experience is here now, but like all these insights and realisations, they are only really experienced when they are new, while the state or experience is still separate. Once you/I become it, there is no more experience as there is nothing to feel. There is just being what I am; but what am I? I now know there is nothing here! 'I', the bit asking the question, is the bit that remains to be dissolved. When this has gone there will be nothing left. So we return again to the apparent fact that there are no answers, beyond the knowledge that nothing exists here. There is only being.

I will try to explain the above further, but I am aware whatever I say is likely to be repeating what has already been said, if worded in a slightly different way.

You think you are here. In fact it could be said you know you are here. This begins when a baby is born and it sees a world full of objects. It soon learns about its own existence through the pains and experiences. It sees all the objects, sees it has a body, feels and experiences through the body and assumes therefore that it must be the body. This is also reinforced by all the other bodies claiming that they are bodies. However, for the individual this is still only a learned assumption; in the same way that when asleep in bed dreaming, no matter how vivid your dream and how much at the time you would say it is real, the fact remains it is still only a dream. Furthermore, it is only the images of the dream that give you the illusion of existing. Take the images away, like in deep, dreamless sleep, and you have no knowledge at all of your existence. You only exist because your surroundings exist, and that includes the body you are dreaming you have. Taking the dream story further, you wake from your dream, see more images in your bedroom and, whilst accepting that before it was only a dream no matter how real it was, you confidently assume this must be real. In fact the only constant in both places is the being or mind that is creating both dreams: you! So we come back to the same question: 'What am I?'

Sorry. The self-knowledge doesn't seem to go beyond the experience of being the intelligence behind all that is, with the knowledge that anything that exists cannot be real since it must have come from somewhere; so the only reality is the point before anything exists. That is the state this intelligence is returning to or, to take a scientific perspective, the point before the 'Big Bang'. But what is the intelligence? We call it God, Allah, Cosmic Consciousness, Universal Mind, amongst other things, but this does not answer the question. It seems there are no answers. I (you) am left with the fact that 'I' am here and can only live and enjoy the formal life amongst the shapes and images as it presents itself, until the images stop and 'I' am no more.

54

☯ ॐ ✡ ☸ ☪ ✝

In Christianity we are taught of an evil personality called the Devil, in conflict with God, causing mayhem and destruction. Some take the story literally. Most believe it is nothing more than a story.

Here I look into the myth behind the story, seeing if there is any truth to it at all.

Does the Devil Exist?

…and if so, who is he?

The story I heard about Lucifer – the Devil – and where he came from explains that he was the closest angel to God and the most powerful. Lucifer had the idea that he could do a better job than God so God sent him to earth to allow him to have a try. And here we are. So, how does this relate in truth to the state of Enlightenment?

If we take the definition of the Devil to be the one who believes he can do a better job than God, look around you. First you may notice the mess the world is in, with all the violence, pain and suffering, the anger and hatred, fear and sorrow. This is indeed a world of pain. Then look at yourself. Look to see if you ever get angry, frightened, resentful or jealous. Look to see if you judge others and yourself, and if you believe you could do a better job than what is already here. Have you ever asked 'Why does God allow this?' and wondered how you could improve things here?

To me, there are only two things here. There is the intelligence or 'being' behind all that is, which we may call God, and then there is the emotion that runs our lives, controlling our thoughts and fears. It is the emotion that separates us from God, which is why Enlightenment has been described in some teachings as 'having no emotional attachments, wanting nothing, and being in the moment and "at one" with God'.

I therefore suggest that if the Devil exists, it can only be in the form of emotion as that is all that is separating you from God; and that is what directs your thoughts, causing you emotional pain and

55

suffering. If you accept this then the Devil is in you as emotion. It behaves like a living entity and we must be very alert and conscious to restrict the amount it controls our thoughts and actions.

In the 'spiritual life' as I teach it, the idea is to become conscious and aware enough through stilling the movement of the mind to deny the emotion – or the Devil within – from expressing itself, and take its power. As the power is reclaimed by the individual, and the emotion – or the Devil and its wish to be separate – is dissolved, the experience of 'God Realisation' comes. That is the knowledge and experience that my being, whatever it is, is God. When the experience is a constant state of being aware that 'I' am the intelligence creating all that is, that is called Enlightenment.

So we have the Devil, struggling to maintain separation from God, striving and fighting with all that is and blaming and accusing, hoping and fearing (as ultimately he has no power at all other than what he is given) and as time passes he weakens. The intelligence of God, which is his own source, begins to push through the hard exterior. The Devil continues to fight, but is worn out through fighting all the time and eventually must surrender to God's will.

I say I am Enlightened. I say that I have reached the level of Self-knowledge where everything around me is my own reflection. 'I' am the source of all that is and I am God Realised. However, I must ask, 'Truly who or what is God Realised?' I have said there is only God and the Devil (the emotion) here and that you must be separate from something to experience it. I am the one who is aware that I exist so I am separate, and 'I' am being reduced daily as circumstances result in more emotion being faced and I grow in consciousness and 'self'-knowledge. I am aware that eventually I will have no awareness of my being, as to truly be 'one' means there is no separation. Therefore ultimately there will be no sense of being as there is nothing to reflect off. I say 'I am God Realised', but I see I must also in truth be behind the myth of the Devil, for who or what else can realise God but the one that is separate from God? There is no one else here.

If you understand everything in these pages, better still, everything ever written on Enlightenment, will you be Enlightened? Here I explain the difference between knowing something in your own experience and understanding it.

Self-knowledge Versus Understanding

It is very easy to allow the mind to try to understand everything. It will try to work everything out, and from its interpretation of its understanding will form an idea as to what is being said. It will then claim to 'understand', but that is not knowledge. With regards to self-knowledge, this comes from the experience of watching and learning. Intellectual understanding will not bring about self-knowledge.

To make this clearer, I will liken it to learning to surf...A person can read every book ever written on how to surf. They may meet the world's greatest surfers, discuss their different techniques, debate which is the most efficient method and maybe years later write their own, very good book on how to surf, all without ever having set foot on a surf board. The first time they do try for themselves, to their surprise they fall off immediately.

I am going to suggest you do *not* try to understand what is here, or what any Master has said. You will get tied up in debates as to who said what, with all the discussing and questioning. You need (if I may say so) to experience it for yourself and not just understand it.

As far as I can see, amongst the constants in all the teachings I've come across are the instructions: 'Be where you are now. Learn to stop questioning and trying to work everything out, and just be what you are.' I say that the more emotion you can dissolve through facing it and not feeding it by reliving the problem in your imagination, the easier it is to be where you are. It is the emotion driving the imagination. Denying the imagination and dissolving the emotion will reveal the truth to you and then it will be your own truth,

57

not what you understand of what someone else said; or even something they may *not* have said, as many of the teachings have been handed down over centuries, being misquoted and altered.

So, I suggest you get on the metaphorical surfboard, fall off a few times and ask a Master (if you have access to one and you do now) how to stay up longer. This way you will grow in self-knowledge and no amount of debating will take away from you what you have experienced. You will soon not be following anybody else, or trying to fit what one person said with what another said. Everything will be in your own experience. Eventually you will be surfing easily, meeting your own new challenges with different waves. There will be no one to ask and no need to ask anyone. You will be the Master of your own board. Otherwise, if you were to use your mind to try to work it all out, even if my words or the words of another Master were clear enough and your brain sharp enough, to enable you intellectually to understand the experience of Enlightenment, you would not be Enlightened. You must drop the trying to understand and use the energy to be where you are, to see what you see, feel what you feel, do what you do and think and imagine as little as possible. This will bring you closer to what you are looking for; closer to being what you are behind what you think you are. Enlightenment must be lived, not understood.

These days we look to science more and more to explain the workings of the universe; to offer some reason as to why we are here? Can science really give the answers we crave?

Can Science Save Us?

Science is truly a wonderful subject, exploring the mechanics of the physical world. It prides itself on being based on facts. One fact supports the next, each a new discovery bringing us closer to the overall picture where all will be known.

Science makes our civilised way of life possible with all the technologies. We live longer due to the knowledge of anatomy and the medical advances push to greater achievements daily. Our knowledge and understanding of the world in which we live is amazing compared with what we knew and were able to do only a hundred years ago; barely more than one generation.

However, no matter how many certain facts one has, if the starting point is only an assumption it brings all that follows into question. I am going to say what the assumption is, and it is so deeply seated into each of us that the mere suggestion that it may not be the case can seem ridiculous, and even laughable. Here goes...

Science, and indeed our entire outlook on life, is based on the assumption that everything around me/you exists before I/you do. That is to say, the world is here and I am born into it. I walk around and interact with it as I do and when I die it continues to remain without me. The assumption is that the people left behind may or may not manage without me, but nevertheless everything exists whether I am here or not and that the world is independent of me. I am suggesting to you that this is not the case.

Enlightenment gives the self-knowledge that there is indeed an intelligence behind all that is, and amazingly it is my own intelligence. I (this being I am) am creating everything each and

59

every moment. Nothing exists unless I am here to experience it. Indeed I am creating it to experience it. When I say 'I', I am of course talking from <u>your</u> experience. The being in you is what you call 'I'.

So 'I' am first. I, whatever 'I' am, am the source of all that is. When I am not here, nothing is. I create the universe each and every moment, but not the universe in some far-off galaxy. We are talking about what is here, now, in your own sensory experience. The knowledge is that there is nothing beyond my own senses, because I have not created it yet. (I know this is deep, and perhaps to some 'crazy talk', but just look at it if you can.)

So, scientists are trying to work out the universe; pulling apart and dissecting atoms, finding more and more 'nothing' the deeper they go, and yet they find increasingly how things seem to be interconnected somehow. They look to find the moment before the 'Big Bang', how it all began and where everything came from. The more answers they seem to find, the more questions they seem to uncover. Is there no end?

The answer to this question is of course, no! No matter how many discoveries the scientific world makes, they will never find the answer. The reason is, as I said, they base all their investigations on the basic assumption that the world was here before they were born, before they (the individual scientist) existed. They are looking in the wrong place if they want to find the truth!

If the individual (you) is experienced enough, one day you will have had enough of searching through all the stuff around you for answers and may look within at yourself. Here you will discover (if you haven't already) that you are not separate; that this space you have taken for granted your whole life, this space that is your very being, is the source of all that you see and experience. You, this being that you are, are the centre of the universe, and the space you feel is the point before time began; the point before the 'Big Bang' theory.

Science will never know this, as science is about measuring and experimenting what is 'outside' in the physical word. Only the individual, whether scientist or civilian, can know this truth; and only through self-knowledge within his or her own experience can

60

anything be known. It cannot be proven. It can barely be explained (as you can see here), but that doesn't mean it's not the truth. It just means it's not accessible to everyone all the time, but only because he or she isn't ready to see it. Not because it isn't there. The truth really is within you. It's not 'out there' at all.

There seems to be some dispute amongst spiritual teachings and philosophies as to whether or not there is free will. Here are my own insights into the subject.

Free Will

It seems to me that the term 'free will' – which is a fact – is confused with the terms 'free choice', 'free action' and even 'free thought', which are all myths.

Free will is the movement or urge to be separate from the whole, but it has no power separate from the whole except for the urge to be separate. This movement is expressed as shapes, images and sensations, which all appear separate to the 'free will', and enable it to entertain itself amongst these forms while thinking it's free. The truth is, it isn't free at all, and all the forms and feelings are still within the whole, as is its own being. Nothing's separate.

It thinks it has free choice, but its choices are limited to its imposed environment, as are its actions; and even its thoughts, which come from its own depths as images and ideas, are either given or not given according to the experience it needs. Eventually the strength of the will to be separate and independent weakens as it grows tired of the constant battle over its environment, and it begins to look to be united again.

The 'spiritual life' is the process of focusing on, or becoming aware of, the space between and around the objects (and feelings) more and more, growing in the knowledge that all is connected and I (the free will) am not separate at all. Eventually all movement or desire to be separate will have been satisfied. Then there is no more 'free will' and no more shapes, or feelings even, leaving only the potential for it to begin again. Hence we have the cycle of life manifesting into existence and out again (or, as described in the Bhagavad-Gita, the holy book of the Hindu religion, the God Brahman as he breathes existence out and inhales again).

☯ ॐ ✡ ☸ ☾ ✝

Whilst out walking in the woods looking at the leaves falling from the trees, it occurred to me the essence of life could be likened to a tree, using the leaves to symbolise individual bodies. Here is this story of life and existence, as likened to a tree expressing itself through its leaves.

The Tree of Life

The leaf had awareness of itself, but no knowledge of the branch or tree it was attached to. It saw other leaves all around it and discussed with them the nature of things and how they came to be.

As time passed and the leaf saw other leaves grow old and eventually die and fall to the ground, it became afraid of its own eventual demise. It would discuss with other leaves about life after death and reincarnation etc and mourn after lost friends.

The form of the leaf could not be sustained indefinitely and soon it too became old and died, and with it died its memories, feelings, beliefs and opinions. All that was left of the leaf and its life was the need to exist, as a new bud and a new leaf grew in its place to continue the cycle where the other had left off.

After a while, the need which had created the leaf in the first place also began to diminish. It had existed in the forms of so many leaves and each had struggled as a separate entity through so much, looking outwards for the answers. At last the leaf began to turn its attention inwards, towards the essence of its being and where it came from. It became aware it was part of something greater. It became aware of the branch it was on, and later aware that it was actually part of the tree the branch was on.

The insights deepened and soon the little leaf had the knowledge that, not only was it a part of this great tree, but in essence it *was* the tree. Its awareness was still in the body of the leaf, but now it knew its own being was the very energy behind all the leaves, and not just the one it seemed to be in. As it saw this, it

63

lost all fear of dying as it knew it could not die. It was, after all, the tree creating all the leaves, and the tree had always been here. It was the tree that gave life to all the leaves.

But what was this tree? Where did it come from? When in the knowledge of the tree the being found that it had no awareness of anything. It was only as a separate form, such as the leaf, that its being could be known at all, and the leaf found there was no knowledge beyond this. It found there were no answers beyond the knowledge and experience that its own being, as the tree, was the source and essence of all leaves. (This is the religious dilemma: If God made the world, who made God?)

So the leaf reached what we call Enlightenment, where it was in the experience of being the one being behind all the other bodies, and yet still had no knowledge of the source of this being. The leaf was now no longer just a leaf. From outside perception it still had the body of a leaf and it lived the life of a leaf, but it lived in constant connection with a feeling of completeness that came from being in union with the source of all leaves. In truth it was actually the tree expressing itself through a leaf.

As this experience deepened, the need for the leaf to be a separate form diminished and then was gone. The leaf was now the tree. From the outside perception it could be said the leaf fell to the ground and died, but really it did not die and it could not fall. There was no leaf and without the leaf there was no tree to fall from, as the tree did not exist without the leaf through which to experience itself. Thus we have the immortality of consciousness. The Enlightened person, the Master consciousness, cannot die. Existence simply ends; for a while at least.

Quite a bold title and the result of an insight which I had in 1999, a long time before it became a living experience here. This is just as I wrote it then and describes the process of how the space of intelligence (God) came to create existence; and how and why it will cease, to begin again.

The Mind of God

There was a space of pure intelligence. Within it there grew a need for some experience. This need created the illusionary world. The illusion was its own Being, its own unconscious mind creating its surroundings every moment. The reason for experience was the reason for existence in the first place, so the being relished in every opportunity. It looked forward to the next experience and this looking forward created a separation between itself and its own unconscious mind.

For a while this would be a little uncomfortable as it had let go of the feeling of being complete and whole. However, it knew this would be made up for when the event arrived and it would be able to enjoy it in the moment, thus being complete again. This created a positive edge to the feeling. It knew that it would soon be reunited again in the moment and the feeling would be wonderful. The anticipation of this would grow stronger as the event drew nearer.

When something was absent (somebody left or died etc), again it let go of the moment to look back into its secondary imagination, remembering the object. This letting go of its own unconscious mind again gave it the feeling that something was missing. In its ignorance it thought this was the object, not stopping to realise it was because it had let go of its own truth, its own knowledge that it was behind everything. It felt incomplete because it WAS incomplete!

Through its own unconscious mind, the being got what it wanted. It wanted feeling and experience, so that was what it got. Situations would happen, people would come and go, just to

65

give it the feelings it sought. The more it enjoyed these feelings, the more it had! The being was spending all of its time thinking now about past and future, very rarely conscious at all of its missing half so always feeling incomplete. When remembering something that had gone forever, it felt negative as it knew it would never have the experience of being with that object to make it whole again. When thinking about an oncoming event, it often looked forward to it because it knew that would give it the feeling of completeness it required.

As soon as it was reunited with its being again and was complete in the moment, it would quickly find, after the initial impact, that there was actually no feeling here at all. Unable to stand this for long, off it would go again in its quest for feeling, by thinking of other times and places to increase the experience in the moment.

There are other occasions when the being gets such a strong feeling from being somewhere or doing something that it is unable to think about anything else. In these instances it can feel whole or free and even 'Enlightened'. These are times which require great concentration, especially involving personal risk, and there is no space for the mind to move and the being feels 'at one', for a while.

The more the being uses its imagination, the more it is separated from its unconscious where it is complete and the stronger the feelings get. The unconscious creates situations 'outside' with the sole purpose of causing a feeling inside. People die, cars crash, people leave, all to bring up some feeling. After some time of this, the being may begin to wonder: 'What is it all about? Why are things so painful?'

If it is earnest in its desire to no longer have all the ups and downs, its unconscious as usual brings to it what it wants. The being is now taught how to identify no longer with feelings, but instead to remain conscious of its own being in the moment as much as possible. This is, of course, extremely hard. It seems almost impossible not to get sucked into the feelings which were its constant companion for so many years. With practise and its distaste of negativity becoming stronger, it gets easier, and the being comes to know again the wonder of being complete; but this time it is a

66

constant state with no comings and goings or ups and downs. Life seems to work out for the best every time. When a situation occurs that would usually provoke a feeling, the being remains conscious, denying the movement. As a result fewer situations are created as they are no longer required to stimulate the being's feelings.

The being now knows the truth again and yet is still within its illusionary existence. It has not yet satisfied its need for experience and continues to enjoy its world in a state of fullness and completeness. It is no longer separated from its knowledge by situations. All are solved quickly and without effort as its physical life continues to unfold every moment.

The being becomes more and more engrossed in the feeling of being complete and less concerned with the illusion around. Eventually the need for experience will have been satisfied and the illusion will end; the complete being once again settling into a state of just pure intelligence with no need for feelings or sensations of any kind...

...until the next time!

A family friend studying the subject 'the theory of knowledge' for her A levels had to look at the following question and asked me for my input (October '03). Here is my answer. She (and her class) said it offered a new perspective and it seemed worth including here.

How Do I Know I Know I Know?

'You asked me the question "How do I know I know I know?". The truth is, I don't really know anything except that 'I am!'. Our usual knowledge is a combination of memories and past experiences and we then use them to make assumptions about the present and the future.

I may say that 'I know' there is a wall in front of me. However, science tells us that everything is due to electrical impulses translated by the brain. Also the atoms that make up the physical world are largely (totally?) just energy, so I can even question the truth behind the wall.

My experience tells me what the wall means to me – that is, I must walk round it, it is good for hanging pictures on etc – and while this continues to be the case I will continue to say 'I know this'. I am aware, though, that this is just an assumption. Just because the wall has always behaved in a certain way, can I really say 'I know' it always will?

Taking this further, I may say that 'I know' what is in the room next door because I was there a few minutes ago and have been there a thousand times, and it has always been the same. The truth is, though, I am not in that room now; I am here. I do not know what is in that room, or even that it exists at all, until I go there. Again, the only true knowledge I have is the ability to reflect on my being and know that 'I am now'. Whatever 'I' may be or ultimately 'where' I may be, 'I am'!

The friend included the above 'as is' in her essay for college, and below it wrote the following…

68

'I loved reading this. It gave me such an insight to another perspective on knowledge and I find it extremely plausible. It so completely changed my views on everything that I have learnt that in the end I believe that we only have assumptions of knowledge. I have no argument to attack this with, no other opinions because essentially it is all completely true. I feel that on the small scale everything can be linked to the theories mentioned earlier [in her essay] but on the much, much larger scale, there is no way to prove that your proof is even true.

In conclusion I feel that simplistically everything can be proven to be true, but realistically nothing can be proven to exist.'

I received an email from a regular contact who has had some good insights. His opening line was 'I recently saw a cool movie called *Vanilla Sky*. If you have seen it, then you would know that you are my "Tech Support"...' This seemed like a pretty good title for a page.

Tech Support... Vanilla Sky

The truth is...yes, I am!

You have heard it said that this is all a dream, an illusion, 'Maya' (using an Eastern term). Well, if this is true, whose dream do you think it is? God's? Well, yes, that would be true, but where is God now? Lost in his/her/its dream perhaps? Like you?

I am indeed your Tech Support here and now. There may be others in the form of other Enlightened persons, such as figures in Buddhist stories and other Enlightened teachers, all telling you to wake up as you are dreaming and are not really here etc. Well, I am here to see if I can clear a few things up.

It is true this is a dream; a wonderful dream where all is possible, both good and bad and all areas in between. The dream is that you are separate and that you must work and strive to survive, as you look to fill the void inside where you feel at times there is something missing. You wonder and question what it's all about and hope there is a purpose to it. You may even look to 'Enlightenment' to solve everything, as you have heard it is to be 'at one' with the universe, to realise 'God' and be beyond time and space and even death. Can anybody help?

So, here I play the role of Tech Support and offer to assist you, first by telling you: 'You do not have to wake up, or be Enlightened!' Just as in the movie where the Tech Support gave Tom Cruise the choice, you too have the choice. And what's more, here it is not a one time 'decide now or go back to sleep' offer. It is with you each and every moment.

70

Imagine for a moment that in the movie the 'programmers' had decided his dream was going wrong and had gone ahead and pulled the plug without asking him first. Imagine that despite how difficult it all was, suddenly he awoke in the future to find the last years had not been real. He saw that he had died a long time before and had been kept alive in a machine and now they had decided to wake him up. It may have been okay, but it may have been too much. It was indeed better to give him the choice, to tell him while still in the dream that this pain is not real and there is another place, should you want it.

This is your creation and for now you have so far 'chosen' to remain asleep, enjoying the appearance of being separate. When you have had enough of being 'lost' in your dream, you will begin to see through the surface illusion to see it is not so real. In this case, instead of a machine creating this for you, it is your own consciousness/mind and as such you are indeed in control; if not consciously then unconsciously. When you are awake 'enough' you will know this is all your creation, but even then you are likely to want to remain here, dream or not. You will see that whatever it is in you that is creating this continues to create it after you are 'awake' until you no longer need it. Nothing is taken until it's time. No one is going to 'pull the plug' on you. (This is true even if your 'dream' ends before you wake up. You have heard from stories of reincarnation. The dream continues as long as it is needed. Nothing is lost.)

So, please don't worry about not being awake, about being asleep, and about all these teachers and even some pretenders telling you to wake up. Why should you? This is your dream. Why should you wake up until you are ready? Enjoy it as you wish.

You may also see that if this is indeed your dream then you have created all these types to tell you these things, but that's another matter. As I said, you can have whatever you want. This is your life, your dream, and all's well here. You may enjoy it as long as you wish in whatever way you do. I am.

A poem from a visitor to the website:

Dear Nick. I have just been looking at your website and, as sometimes happens, stillness produced a poem – so it's really yours. Trust it comes in handy, somehow, somewhere. *Nosce te ipsum.* JC

Terror

Terror is fear – fear now of me,
Me on my own – or me that I see…
The projection of fear outwardly
That's what's reflected – that terrifies thee.

Terror – the fleeing from what is unkind
But the terror pursues – being locked in the mind.
Terror is the state I can find myself in.
The fear of destruction, pain and such things,
Whence comes the fear that terrorises me?
From the sight of the pain that terror can see.

What is the terror that lurks in the night?
It's the demons within – thought making fright.
Thoughts from the deep, from the Hell within me,
Confusion in Heaven about all I believe.
What is belief? – thought thinks in its way,
I'm safe in the truth – the light of the day.

So in the light of the day terror subsides,
It can't get a grip in being inside.
For the motion of me keeps terror away
But I can't watch forever – being awake.
Terror slips in through moments off guard,
Disturbing the peace – call Scotland Yard!
But police cannot help in policing the mind,
Life on its own must face why I'm blind.

So what is the cure for terror in space?
Is it knowledge? Knowing? Hiding my face?
Is it truth? God? Drink? or pleasures replace?
Passions? Death? Escape to some place?
…Silence.

Then came the silence – the stillness of mind.
Life sees what is good – and accepts what it finds,
Reason replaces reasons – peace is the state,
And I learned how That loves – and how being creates.
Terror is gone – consigned to the bin,
And a smile breaks out – it all came from within.

Thank you for this gift. The truth is within the writer/reader of this piece. I act only as mirror for what is already here. Nick Roach

Truth of Love

Love is an area that many teachers avoid, while some teach celibacy or total promiscuity to find the truth of it. There seems to be little by way of middle ground, so here I describe my own perspective on love, the making of love and the living of love in an everyday relationship, as it deepens in my own life.

This page is to explain a little about what love really is and why it makes us feel the way we do.

What Is Love?

Our experience of love is that it hurts. We long to be with the ones we love and mourn when they are gone. The ones we love seem to give us pain as we fall in and out of love and argue and fight. We see this going on all around us amongst loving couples, friends and families, and everyone seems to accept this as natural behaviour. So why does love hurt? It would almost seem to be a perverse joke.

Well, it isn't a joke. It is self-inflicted due to our ignorance as to what love is, and how it works.

You may have read in earlier pages that there is indeed one being here behind all the forms and the state of Enlightenment is to be united with this knowledge and experience. Before a person reaches this state, everything is still separate. They walk around seeing all these objects and have no idea that they are from their own being. The person sees something or someone they love and feels complete. What happens is the object or person is reflecting a part of the being back to the viewer, putting them in touch with a part they had lost touch with. Hence you have the feeling of being complete. Does that make sense?

I have also said that there is no time in the state of Enlightenment. You may recall when you have been with a person you love – possibly in the early stages of the relationship – there was a knowledge or sensation that this could last forever; that it would be good if you both never had to move again. That's love. Love is being in touch with the moment now, with your own being, and being complete.

So why does love hurt?

When the person we love leaves our immediate experience, we feel we miss the person. We feel we are incomplete without them

77

and long to be with them again. The truth is, we don't miss them at all. What we miss is the feeling of being complete that we get from their reflecting our being/love back to us.

So how do we stop this?

The purpose of the 'love' experience was to put you in touch with a part you had lost, so you could keep it and become more whole; not so you could latch on to the object reflecting it. So when the person has gone, if we hold back the urge to imagine being with them, with their form, and instead take a moment to feel still inside our own being, we will find the feeling of being complete is still there. Nothing has really gone at all. The love they put us in touch with is exactly where they left it. The trouble is our attention can only focus on one thing at a time. If we choose to leave the moment now, to leave the feeling of being complete and instead go into our imagination to think about the object or person, of course we will feel there is part of us missing, as we have let go of it.

So, by holding on to the knowledge that you love the person instead of thinking *about* them, you always feel complete and never miss them; not because you don't love them, but because you do! You will see that you only miss someone when you have actually stopped loving them consciously and have instead started thinking about them and how you are separate from them; and you know this because you feel there is a part of you missing. This is, of course, far removed from our normal way of life. But then our normal way of life is pain and struggle.

Very few people are likely to agree with the above. But unless these people are never unhappy, I would say they are only defending their right to be emotional, to be unhappy and to be separate; and that's okay with me. We all have the right to be separate. That's why the world is here.

☯ ॐ ✡ ☸ ☪ ✝

Enlightenment, it is said, is to be in a state of love. However, little is spoken on the subject of love between man and woman with regards to Enlightenment.

Here I will describe what happens, why it can be so hard, how best perhaps to grow and develop through it and even how eventually to make being together a constant pleasure.

Love Between Man and Woman

Usually the state of Enlightenment is associated with celibacy, as Eastern tradition dictates. However, many of the Masters who taught this, it seems, were later found not to have been celibate at all, or at least had great inner struggle as they tried to keep to this. Then there have been some Masters (one particularly famous one) who taught quite the opposite: that it is good and right to be promiscuous, to have multiple partners and to engage in various sexual activities to express yourself and the emotional drive for more excitement. So what is the truth?

The truth, as is so often the case, is neither of the two extremes. It is true that when talking of sex it is arguable in some cases that it would be preferable to remain celibate rather than indulging in the alternative available. However, there is a very definite difference between sex and Making Love, which few Masters seem to have acknowledged.

Sex (to me) is the emotional drive, the separation from one's being at its most powerful, expressing itself and its need to become complete again through merging with another. This involves taking for oneself with little or no regard for the other. Making Love is in practice very different, but when the term is commonly used it is describing having sex with someone we love, and as we are all so emotional anyway no one knows any different. As a result the man has lost his ability to love the woman and she has to make do with the emotional substitute, or withdraw totally in some deep knowledge that this is not right and that this is not what she wants.

So what is making love? Making love is where the man is there consciously to give the woman pleasure, not through any learnt technique but simply by loving her. He is not rushed, not impatient, and is not looking for his orgasm because that is not loving her. To look for anything beyond what is now is to be unconscious, and that is selfish and is not love. The orgasm will occur if and when it does, but it is not the aim. Being conscious is the aim. Love is consciousness. Consciousness is love.

The aim for the man is to love the woman; to love her enough that she opens up psychically, surrendering to the conscious love. She is not there to please him sexually or for him just to entertain himself inside her and just use her body for his own gratification. She is only for love if they hope to Make Love. It is man's inability to love her that has made her emotional and drives him to build the world and all it contains. Love must start with him.

Just as our emotions are stored within us until we are free through facing them, each failed love experience is stored within the woman. This usually expresses itself as a hardness or an imbedded emotionality that can strike at him (or indeed at any situation) at any time, but especially at her time of the month when her female energies are at their strongest and the knowledge that he is not loving her rightly is nearest the surface. This may be why some women have such a hard time emotionally with PMT (premenstrual tension). It is the lack of love and emotionality reacting to her purer female energies and consciousness pushing through, and they are alien to each other.

Through loving the woman he is with rightly, without giving into his own selfish emotions or hers and through doing everything for her to love her more, the pains of the past loves and hurts from her previous lovers begin to surface. The emotion will arise and at first she will put it onto him. If they are both aware and strong enough, they will have an intelligent conversation about the source of the feelings and uncover that she was treated badly and how the pain of it is here now, ready to be faced and let go of for good. If she is able,

80

she must hold the knowledge of the situation, feeling the pain within (which would be emotional, but after all this time may also be a physical pain), and face and dissolve the emotion, doing her best not to put it onto the man who is loving her now. He too must be careful not to put the past onto her. When either catch themselves doing this – that is, blaming the other or reacting in the present due to past memories – they must have the presence to state clearly to the other why they reacted, apologise where appropriate and dissolve the emotion within. Both will need to support each other in this, or it can be reduced to the all-too-familiar accusations and judgments which we are looking to be free of.

Depending on the level of commitment in each party, eventually the woman will state that she knows all the past lovers have gone from her. She knows she is free of them finally through the new man loving her rightly (or the old one who has reformed) as he has removed all the pain, all the past hurts, regrets and emotions where she was not loved before. This is man's purpose now. He has left love and woman to build a loveless world and now, if he is ready, it is time to go back: back to the love he came from, the love that created them both, and here they will be together forever in the knowledge that they were never really apart.

The truth of Making Love, with consciousness and not emotion or imagination, is the truth of Tantric love, where each grows in love and consciousness to become free of past emotions, and to become 'one' with their love, both within and without. By contrast unconscious love-making (sex) makes more emotion, more pain, more separation and more problems.

This page looks at how to keep a relationship new and the love real, like it was in the beginning.

Keeping the Love Alive

We are all aware of the sensations of a new relationship. The yearning to be with the other as the centre, and perhaps even the entirety, of your world, in the feeling that you can't get enough of them is commonplace at the beginning. It is as if you could lie together holding one another forever and ever. And time seems to stand still when you are apart, as the pain of missing the other pulls as a constant reminder that you are separate from the one you love. The frequently heard expression is, 'Ah, young love. It won't last, you know!' But you feel you know it will last. Nothing can separate you and nothing will take away this wonderful experience you share. At least, that's how it feels.

Sure enough, it is not long before the pain of separation when you are apart has indeed gone, but with it so has something else. The moments together don't seem to be special any more, as the everyday living takes over and you settle down into the routine. One person does these chores while the other does those. Perhaps you manage to eat a meal together in front of the television in the evening after work and before going to bed, often barely speaking, occasionally arguing. I have even heard a saying 'When the ring goes on the finger, the sex goes out the winda' and there is a truth in this, as often something has died in the relationship as a whole, as well as in the sex life. After some time, if sex happens at all it is often more of a routine, or even an inconvenience, compared with the passionate love, longing and excitement that were present in the beginning. This process is the accepted way of things here.

What happens next to the couple is this: With the loss of the spark and intensity goes the thrill and enjoyment. We stop making an effort and can even seem to stop loving at all. The living together becomes habitual and more noticeably tension rises, and the environment can become uncomfortable, aggressive and argumentative. We may begin to wonder what we ever saw in the person and perhaps look for a way out. Some may remain in this situation indefinitely, occasionally seeking some comfort in the arms of another; while others may eventually leave to find new love elsewhere, for the cycle to begin again.

You may think the above is a little extreme or that it is spot on. The point is, something seems to have happened to the relationship beyond the 'getting to know each other', as everyday living takes priority over the love which had been everything for a while.

So, can anything be done to break this cycle? Yes! And the answer is in the above words '...everyday living takes priority over the love...'. This is not easy to avoid, but if you are vigilant and work together it can indeed be achieved. Here are a few tips how:

1) Acknowledge and appreciate everything that is done for you, or even the fact that the person is with you at all. All too quickly it is usual to stop saying 'please' and 'thank you', particularly for little things such as receiving a cup of tea. Everything should always be acknowledged and appreciated. You would have done this in the beginning, so why did you stop? The reason is, you stopped because you began to take each other for granted and no one likes to be taken for granted.

2) Make a list, even for fun, of the things you used to do together and have since stopped. This can cover aspects such as going for walks, holding hands, talking to each other, looking at each other, cuddling, saying words such as 'I love you and love being with you'; in fact anything you would do now in a new relationship if you were given the chance. Then look at why you don't do them any more in your current relationship and could you do them again? Is the person you love and are with now not worth this attention any more? Or perhaps you feel you are not worthy of this treatment from the person who is with you and is supposed to love you?

3) Do your best not to put your moods and anger etc onto the other person. No one enjoys being around angry, emotional people and yet we expect our partner to accept being with us when we are

like this. When we have our moods, we don't care whether they enjoy being with us or not. How selfish is that, to decide to be in a bad mood and spoil their enjoyment too, while it suits you? Talk to your partner about this and your reluctance to accept their moods or your own any longer. There is no need to have moods. We accept them as normal, but normal living is not loving-living, is it? That is why the love does not last. Try to hold on to the knowledge inside that the love is more important than whatever frustration you are feeling. I am not saying it's easy, but it must be done as much as you can if you are to stop the love from being covered over.

4) Hold on to the knowledge also that it is love that you want. You are not going to roll over and be anyone's servant or accessory, or however else you may feel you are perceived, other than in love, just for a peaceful life. It will not really be peaceful for you if you do anyway, because you will know you are not loved and you will be disturbed by this. This process does require both parties to make it work, and as you may know by now no matter how much you give, if the other does not want or is unable to meet you half way, it will be an 'uphill struggle'.

So, I say you are not going to accept not being loved. However, I am aware you can only do this to the extent you have had enough of not being loved and to the extent you feel you deserve love. In the end the aim is to know you will not be with a person if they are not prepared to put love first, even above your own selfishness, if it emerges. Controversially this may mean being prepared to put the knowledge and the need of love before the personal likes and dislikes, theirs and yours, with neither party making a stand any more than necessary. Remember how it was in the early days when you both would have agreed to just about anything as long as you were together. We are looking to bring the love of those days back, without necessarily having to start a new relationship. It probably wouldn't last anyway, unless you worked hard at keeping that one new, as the same mistakes are likely to be made if lessons are not learned beforehand.

5) This next tip is very tough (perhaps especially so in this modern world), but it can also be the part that makes or breaks the

84

relationship. That part is honesty. First, I propose the apparently unusual idea that to be honest with someone you need to actually be aware of the person you are with while you are with them, and not always drifting off, imagining being somewhere else with somebody else (sound tough?). How can you claim to be honest with someone when you are not even able to hold your attention on them for more than a few minutes before drifting off in another personal world? If my body is with you then I will make sure my mind is too. I will not allow myself to be in two places at once. That's the first teaching in honesty, but it isn't easy to practise.

Then there are two other main areas of being honest and true to love.

The first is the subtle but difficult area of not covering over things that disturb you about the other. Each unresolved issue is a crack between you that is covered over and grows beneath the surface. If something disturbs either of you, there needs to be an agreement that it will be brought up and addressed at the time, but if that is not possible, then as soon as is possible afterwards. This is not a 'witch hunt' or a battle to blame and accuse, but simply a means to ensure there is nothing separating you that has not been acknowledged and addressed. The more you find you are able to express the slightest disturbance without any judgement, the more you can work as a team to combat the emotion that would end the love.

The last area of honesty is of course the big one and the area we are all familiar with. That is of telling the truth and not covering up something or avoiding the question. One sure way to destroy a relationship is with lies and secrets. Each time this occurs it is another area of separation: another part of you or your life you cannot share with the person you are supposed to love and who loves you. If your partner will not share with you what s/he is doing or feeling or thinking, you will know the feeling of separation that occurs: the doubt and lack of trust. If it is you doing the covering up and you regard it as only a small thing, then why lie about it or hide it? Why is it worth separating from your love psychically for such a small thing?

If, however, it is a big thing, what then? Well, if you know your partner would most likely not want to be with you any more if they knew what you had done (for example), then from that day on your life together is based on a lie; isn't it?! Imagine you find out something about your partner weeks, months or even years down the line – that they had betrayed you, for example, and had lied about it ever since. You knew they had carried it with them every day and in all the conversations since when you had spoken about honesty and love they had looked you in the eye and lied. How would you feel? In fact how do you feel, because very likely it has happened to you at some time. You are likely to feel your last few weeks, months or years have been taken away from you. You may even feel you could have dealt with it at the time, had you been given the opportunity, or maybe you couldn't have. Either way, you now know your idea or view of the person you had been with all this time doesn't exist and it can feel like having to start the relationship again, as if you have to get to know them all over; and you may ask yourself the question, is it worth it?

You can see from the above how another person is likely to feel if they find you have been lying to them, however small the issue may be, and how perhaps they would have a right to expect the same level of honesty from you. Honesty is vital if you are going to put love first. This does mean, of course, you must love each other enough to limit the emotional response and be strong enough to handle the truth, even if it means leaving in the end.

When I talk of honesty, I do not talk of the common aspect 'trust' because that comes with time. I suggest you really want to <u>know</u> the person and not 'blindly' trust them just because you feel you love them. If you know that they may let you down, at least it isn't a shock when it happens, and perhaps you can both learn and grow if you choose to stay together. More importantly, as time passes and you both find out that the other has lied on occasions, through fear of what would be said regarding an action (for example), you come to see that the problem is usually in the lie itself and the reasons why this was deemed necessary, and not necessarily in the action. Knowledge builds trust and the fear starts to fall away.

86

6) This piece is entitled 'Keeping the Love Alive'. In this society this often includes sex, but I am not referring to sex; I am referring to love. It is commonplace that we are taught how to excite and entertain each other, to keep the desire and the wanting strong. I am not looking to teach you how to keep your man excited and dying to sleep with you all the time. Neither am I looking to teach the man how to get the woman excited and to have many orgasms. Believe it or not that would not be love, despite what we are taught. Both would be looking for their own sexual release and you know by now that that is not love. Likewise, satisfying the woman with strong stimulations and emotions is exciting to both, but excitement always ends. We are looking for lasting love here and becoming 'one' together as a living constant experience and no longer the emotional rollercoaster ride we are used to.

This next area on sex and Making Love may be new to you, to both of you, and is related to point '5' of being conscious while together physically: He needs to stay aware of the woman he is with, as well as of himself, and of the fact that he loves her. He is there to love her and not just to please himself or entertain their emotions. He must stay aware and remain conscious of her and her body, so he is not carried away to be lost in his own sexual excitement. The woman needs to do the same, acknowledging and appreciating the man she is with, and not allowing herself to drift off in some self-contained emotional euphoria. She can teach him how to touch her, how to acknowledge and appreciate her, but she must ensure that she stays with him and doesn't allow herself to drift off either. This is about you two becoming one, not about two people in their own imagination and excitement using each other's bodies for their own enjoyment. Stay with it. Work together.

It may be that you have been together so long that there seems to be no real spark or love left in the love-making – or even in the idea of it. Alternatively, for the man, it may be that he is sometimes hurried as he wants to get there, or he may be working hard to contain his excitement by thinking about something mundane like the football scores etc. You know this is also not love. How can it be, if his mind is on something other than loving the woman he is with?!

87

The more he is able to remain conscious of being with her in the room, and that he is there to please her by loving her and not just to please himself, the more she will feel truly loved and appreciated; and the more he will enjoy true love-making. The energies transferred in conscious love-making are the truth behind the myth of 'Tantra' and will bring the man and woman together in love. Sex, in the form of personal sexual excitement and gratification, even when shared with another, is still excitement and does not last. Excitement always ends and always wants more stimulation to get the same high. The more you get, the more you will want and need. If you can put love first, you will find love is always enough. In fact the love is everything.

7) The last tip here is the summary of all the above. There is an old saying: 'You don't know what you've got until it's gone.' This is very true, but perhaps even sadder is the point that when we do get it back, we are prone to taking it for granted again. If you really want to keep love alive, you do need to appreciate and acknowledge it, in whatever form it's in. If you are the one not being loved, appreciated and acknowledged, and you now know you do want/need to be, you will not be able to accept it for long. Life is here to be enjoyed and you are here to be loved. As woman you are man's love in form. As man you are woman's. You are each other's greatest pleasure, if you can realise it. Know your own worth and that of your loved one. The more you respect and love each other, the more you find you respect and love yourself, and vice-versa. Emotion breeds emotion, while love and consciousness breed love and consciousness. The choice is there every moment of every day.

There has been a huge increase in spiritual interests in recent years, not least of all when it comes to Tantric sex. The stories focus on sex sessions going on for hours at a time and increased orgasms, as is the way in this world. Here I look further into what true Tantra is all about.

Tantric Love

What is Tantra?
First I am going to describe a little about the difference between making love and sex. This will make explaining Tantric love easy to define.

Love is consciousness (and I explain this more in some detail under the title 'What Is Love?'). This being the case, to 'make love' is to make consciousness. So what is sex?

Sex is a lack of consciousness, just as to be emotional is a lack of consciousness. Sex is the looking for an end, or for something else beyond now, which is a common characteristic of emotion. To be looking for something beyond this moment is obviously not to be fully conscious in this moment, thus we have the simple difference between making love and sex. Physically they may have the same external appearance, but to love is to do the act while being totally aware now, while sex is to think about it and to be lost in the feelings it brings up. So, what do these differences mean to us in practical terms?

As most will know all too well, it is man's way to look for his orgasm. If the woman has one too, that's great, but it's not the purpose of sex for him. It is solely for him to relieve himself and his own tension. Conversely woman's way, if I may say so, would initially be to look for love. That is why we have the beautiful fairytales of the knight in shining armour coming to save her from the evils she endures. However, as each woman has repeatedly experienced man's selfishness and lack of love, she now lives with a constant choice:

1) She can either withdraw from sex totally in all its forms, often with a feeling of disgust and an inner knowledge of the betrayal she faces; or

2) She can allow man to have his way with her, accepting that much of the time it is not satisfactory and will have to leave it at that, or make up for the lack of stimulation with other practices such as masturbation; or finally

3) She can throw herself into sex, with the (possibly subconscious) view 'If you can't beat them, join them', and really look for sexual excitement whenever possible to make up for the lack of love and acknowledgement she feels.

None of the above alternatives are expressions of love, as many are already aware, and therefore they will not set woman free from the emotional trap; but there is another way that does offer the love we crave. It is the act of making love that every woman dreams of, which almost all have long since accepted as fantasy and fairytale.

It is generally accepted that emotion is stored in a person's psyche (or body) and that every hurt and pain is still there, hidden. The spiritual path to Enlightenment is the process of dissolving these past pains, which actually are what drive the thinking mind and are the separation from the Enlightened state. This next bit is almost obvious but may not be popular, since as a society we strongly believe, despite all the evidence to the contrary, that emotion and sex do not do anybody any harm. So here goes:

It has been said, and is commonly accepted, that when a woman has intercourse with a man a connection is made. This is the truth. The psyches do merge (as they become 'as one') and he leaves some non-physical element or imprint of himself within her. Each time a man enters a woman and has sex with her, he is actually increasing her emotionality and lack of consciousness by passing on to her some of his sexual aggression, desire for self-gratification and lack of love. She will know she has not been loved and will carry this and store it with every other hurt she has ever experienced. The woman can be seen to become more emotional,

90

and often even harder and more masculine, the more she has sex with a sexual man, often relative to how sexual and aggressive her partner is. Unfortunately women having multiple partners seems to be the new 'equal opportunities and women's lib': 'Let's be more like men and have as many partners as we can.' Having said that, the need for sex is just the 'need for experience' expressing itself, and the lack of love searching for completeness by joining with another person.

So what is the answer? The answer is in the question 'What is making love?':

If the man resists the excitement and movement of his mind to want to please himself, and instead holds the knowledge that he is there to love the woman and give her pleasure selflessly (and we do not mean to excite her sexually, but to truly love her with patience and conscious awareness of all that he is feeling), then not only is he not increasing the amount of emotion in her body as in sex, but he is actually removing it. This conscious process is truly 'making love', as it is removing the woman's stored emotion from the past sexual partners, where she was not loved, and replacing it with consciousness. This brings the ability in her to feel the peace and stillness to a greater and greater extent. Life becomes easier and she knows she is loved. This will also reduce the sexual excitement in him, as he selflessly gives her pleasure and her renewed consciousness increases his, as his does for her. This way they both grow in love, not excitement.

What are the benefits to this 'conscious sex'? Well, apart from the woman knowing she is loved and therefore becoming less and less emotional, and apart from them both experiencing all new sensations not possible through any physical stimulation (because they are not from the physical, but the conscious exchange of energies), there will also be a reduction of many of the usual 'women's problems', as these are often caused by sexual aggression, emotion and the lack of love destroying her from the inside. This is really nothing too new or extreme, as it is well accepted that stored emotional tension causes physical symptoms.

You may have noticed that in all the above there is no talk of any specific technique. There is no magic position or substance to take or place to go or clothes to wear. There is no belief to have or anything to follow. There is not even anything to want or to try to attain. All that is required is the will to remain as conscious as possible, both the man and the woman loving each other without wanting anything beyond what is now. The man gives the woman pleasure consciously. She opens up psychically to accept this more and more according to how much he can give to her, and this in turn gives him greater pleasure. The more he gives, the more she receives and thus the more he receives; as long as both remain conscious and loving. It takes both parties to do this.

So, to answer the question 'What is Tantra?', true Tantric love is to make love physical, which means to bring love into experience here, thus raising the conscious awareness of both parties and serving to contribute to freeing them from the emotions of the past; taking them nearer to the Enlightened state. Tantra contributes to 'God Realisation' as a constant experience and is not simply about increased orgasms as our sex-obsessed world likes to focus on.

Extra tips...

The biggest tip I can ever give really, on any subject, but perhaps particularly when it comes to making love, is to be aware of where you are and of what you are feeling. This will keep you conscious. A man who allows himself to think and imagine having sex with a woman when he is alone will find he is not able to love her when he actually gets to be with her. He will be too excited to be in the moment with her, and the more sensitive she is, the more she will know that he is not truly loving her. So, to both parties, attempt to limit the amount of imagining you do all through the day. The more you do this, the deeper and more profound the love making becomes. This is Tantric love.

☯ ॐ ✡ ☸ ☪ ✝

As a person goes deeper into the experience of Enlightenment, the position 'I am this' can be a good vantage point from which to see how other aspects relate to each other. That is to say, now I know – and am – the beginning as a living truth, this is a solid foundation from which to follow the established logic to explain the dream further. (Even self-knowledge must still be interpreted by the mind.)

Homosexuality

Part one

Q: Why do you talk about love between man and woman, but not mention homosexuality?

A: First, because I am not homosexual. I write about my personal experiences and insights but my experience with regard to homosexuality is limited, and therefore, perhaps, so is my knowledge. I will say what I can for now and no doubt more will occur with time, because that is how it works. The knowledge and insights do not come all at once.

Those who are born homosexual I will talk about at the end, but it seems many are not born homosexual. The change occurs, perhaps following some bad experiences. Possibly a woman was mistreated by a man or men, and later finds companionship in the arms of another woman in preference to being alone, in the knowledge she does not want to be with a man any more.

On the other side, a man may have had relationships with woman (I will use the term 'woman' to gave name to the essence of woman in one or many forms) and found her too hard to understand and love. He was, after all, trying to love her through his own sexuality and hers, and this came back at him through her emotionality. So again, it became easier to be with another man who would understand his needs and wants, and perhaps they would give each other what they wanted. You may ask then, 'So where is the love in this?'

93

Love is the reflection of one's own being expressed or experienced through another, whether male or female. So the love is the same; love is love. And man's obsession with sex is the same, whether with a woman or another man, so the sex, wherever and however it is expressed (and we know man's sexuality when pushed will go to extremes to express itself), is still sex. We are now left with the subject of making love and how this differs:

To me, making love is to raise the level of consciousness of yourself and the other through consciously loving them. Sex cannot do this. Sex is the destroyer of love in the sense of selfishness and lack of consciousness. Therefore any wanting or trying or self-gratification cannot make love; and this applies to homosexual love or heterosexual love. Sex is sex; it is never love. Many would agree with this when looked at in this way.

In my experience woman, the female essence and form, is my opposite. Her softness of nature and subtleness of energy, as opposed to the male coarseness, is what I am attracted to. It is the essence of the woman I love and something which is perhaps in all women, which is not in man. This may be apparent in varying degrees, depending on the woman's level of love or emotionality. The more emotional and hard she is, often through being denied love throughout her life, the more like a man she could be said to become: sexual, demanding, aggressive and impatient, to name a few characteristics which are common to sex but not to love.

Through making love as I describe it here, I (as man) give her my energies and my being and consciousness (not my sexual, emotional selfishness) and in that she releases her finer energies to me as that is the exchange. Thus we make each other more pure, more whole, just like the Yin-Yang symbol: man and woman, Adam and Eve. The two opposite poles together make up the whole and are inseparable as one cannot exist without the other, and yet in the symbol they are certainly individual: two halves, one life.

Following on from the above, I do not need the energies of another man, as I already have my own. And I would suggest a woman does not need the energies of another woman (if she has been loved rightly), as she also has her own. I would suggest

94

therefore that making love in the way I describe perhaps cannot occur through homosexual love, simply because both parties have the same energies; and yet that is not to deny they may love each other deeply and give each other pleasure sexually. It is only to say that energetically they are the same. Perhaps this is the attraction?

With regards to heterosexuals, this attraction of the opposites may bring them together, but then they proceed to spoil it with sexual wanting anyway. Thus the different, pure and individual energies become more one, not as one love but as one emotion. They remain separate within from their own truth and remain lost and unconscious, with the sex driving for more excitement and experience, taking them further away from the wonder of being complete, both within and without, with their opposite in existence.

So, all I am saying is that sex is different from love, and men are different from women. This seems obvious, but it does seem increasingly to be the case these days that it is not politically correct to suggest people are different, as people can't help but put judgement with the idea: that is, different = inferior. This is unnecessary and ridiculous. Why can't people be different, whether male or female, white or coloured, heterosexual or homosexual, without the mind making judgement? This is a world of opposites. There is no judgement here.

I said I would talk about homosexuals who feel they are born that way. I am not going to suggest they put aside their personal emotional fears, likes and dislikes and try to love a person of the opposite sex, as this would be telling them to go against what they feel they are, or what they wish to do, and that is not my way. I can only say do what you do, and because of the nature of things here you can only ever do what you do. We are here to learn and experience and that is what happens whether we like it or not. I do not honestly know whether there is indeed a 'gene' that determines a person's psychological sexuality (belief in being male or female) or their sexual preference, or whether an Enlightened person would always be able to say that they feel no attachment to being male or female or whatever and that just do what they do, but that is how I am.

(This piece was written several months after the last piece.)

Occasionally I have reason to look at homosexuality. Often this is when receiving questions through the website and this area is becoming increasingly popular these days, as people look for reasons, explanations or justifications for their feelings, thoughts and actions. Here I offer an explanation for the idea and practice, and even the truth, behind homosexuality. Take it or leave it, as you will. To my knowledge this has never been seen or expressed before in this way.

Part two

We have established there is one consciousness or being here and this is neither male nor female, since a form is required to be one or the other and consciousness is behind and beyond all forms. In the point before anything exists there is nothing to even know anything at all, let alone whether it is 'male' or 'female'. Then the dream begins...

The intelligence is now in a world of opposites and even its own dreamt body has an opposite. If it is 'male', its body represents the 'doing' creative but separate part from the whole. This is the part that caused the dream to come to be; the part that looked for experience. The body is muscular, often lean, hard and tough. The general mentality is often not particularly sensitive and the reproductive organs are on the outside, representative of the need and designed to 'thrust out' into existence.

By way of contrast, the female body is softer. It is more subtle, smaller, rounded, not as muscular or hard. It is even said she has one layer of skin less than the male body. She is more sensitive, both physically and emotionally, and has what is known as 'women's intuition'. The female form is designed to receive the 'doing' of the male body into her, receiving the energies and physicality. In reproduction she supports the growth of the new form within her own until giving birth to it nine months later. She also possesses breasts

96

through which to feed the new body from her own. So, we can see the female form represents the spirit, the 'Mother' (Mother Nature), the one supporting all being; while the male form represents the separation and the need to exist and drive into existence and achieve. However, he is always looking to return to her again and unite when possible, so how does this relate to Making Love and sex?

Being separate, the man wants to become whole again. It is in his nature to drive into the world, so he looks for a form to 'drive into', to become one with. The female form is perfectly designed for this, as his genitalia is designed to perfectly fit hers. Likewise, she is also looking to become whole psychically and the male part fitting into hers also makes her feel complete physically. The two energies merge: the 'doing', or creation of separation of the male, with the one sustaining being, accepting the return of a part of itself as the female. The two join and become as one on all levels.

With regard to homosexual love, the two energies are the same: the male and the female. The maleness is still looking to drive out into the world, as that is its nature, and the female is still the receptive form, as this is her nature. The physical forms are still the same as before, so what has changed?

I would suggest a man's wish to love another man sexually is still his own wish to return home: to become Enlightened within himself, so he is again 'one' within (that is, after all, the driving force behind each one of us). Practising being conscious and aware would usually bring this about to a certain extent, even if he was alone. It is just that, instead of only doing it within himself, he is trying to merge with these energies within another man (as heterosexual woman does when she joins with him) as the male body reflects, represents and contains the same male energies in himself. I have heard that some homosexual men are particularly attracted to straight men, which may reinforce this explanation of seeking out the male energies. There are also many very 'feminine' gay men and this may be enough to satisfy the still existing need in the man to join with these energies also, having some of the male and female elements in one place. Where we have a man playing the female role, as is also common, I would suggest there may be the same 'forces' at work here (after all, what other forces are there but the individual's drive to become whole again?). A man is still a man. He looks to become whole, within and without, with both the elements represented by the male and the female. He aims to become as close to these female energies as he can and to do this most men look for the physical form that represents and contains the energies they seek, and try to join with this. However, since the man playing the female role is acting out the female characteristics, this could still be an attempt to connect with the receptive female energies, just like any heterosexual man, but by acting them out rather than joining with them physically. (This is largely speculation, as explained above; just following the established logic. But then so much of the realisation process is following the logic, once one is in the experience of being the truth behind all that is experienced: You just begin to step back and see how things fit together, as best you can.)

So, if we accept the above, there are two reasons why a man may be homosexual, depending on whether he takes the 'male' or the 'female' role. The male role may be looking to unite with the male energies within the body of another man (which is the driving force to become Enlightened within oneself). The 'female' role could also be looking to absorb the male energies from the person playing the 'male' position, but at the same time trying to recreate the female energies by acting them out. Perhaps some may 'swap roles', each taking turns in trying to connect with the maleness by taking the dominant position and with the female energies by taking the receptive role. This would serve to explain all forms of physical love or sex, whether homosexual or heterosexual; all being the search for completeness within one's self.

The above explanation applies between two women also. There is always only the one consciousness, which is neither male nor female, divided into the two opposites here in existence. Whatever is done sexually is an attempt to unite consciously with the truth within one's own being, while joining with the opposite here in existence. I trust it can be seen that there is no judgement in any of the above, just as good an explanation as is available at this time.

98

Pages Written by Sally

My partner, Sally, suggested it would be good if she were to write something about her time with me, about how it differed from previous experiences and to describe her new perceptions on life as she lives the teaching. It may offer another perspective while demonstrating how the teaching does actually work, and is not just intellectual theories, as Sally describes some of her own insights in the early days of our relationship.

Here are several pages written by Sally after being with me for a few months…

♥ Sally's Pages ♥

If you have ever lived with a man you love and it hurts, then you are living with a sexual man.

Life with a Loving Man

Life and love with a loving man does not hurt. It comes so naturally. You do not have to be careful of what you say or what you do for fear of his reaction. If he cannot handle things that have happened to you or something that you have done in the past, then that is his fear and emotion, not yours.

When you start a new relationship it is all so exciting: you cannot wait to be together; you cannot get enough of each other; you can keep talking for hours on end. But all too soon you start to get complacent, take each other for granted and forget about the 'love'. You 'put up' with the moods and emotions from each other, until you forget the reason why it disturbed you in the first place. You stop talking, stop communicating and stop loving. Some people remain in this state for the rest of their lives. They marry and have children in the hope that it will rekindle the spark, but your inner being 'knows' that it is not right. Some stay together but others try to find the 'love' with another, when the truth is the 'love' was there all the time. It is in all women and all men; they have just forgotten that it's there.

The world is built around man's sexual aggression and has invaded the woman of love so much that she accepts it as 'just the way life is'. But life is not meant to be like that and only a loving man can show you how it should be. Emotions, wanting and trying are all man-made and only a man of love can accept that this has been his doing, and that it is his responsibility to put it right. A loving man will respect your feelings but won't accept your emotions. Why should he? They are only a reflection of his own aggression, and if he gets that aggression out of himself, why should he accept it in you?

In love you acknowledge everything that you do for each other, no matter how small. Even just to make a cup of tea, a thank you shows that you appreciate the effort that your partner has put in for you. To make love with a loving man is all you want to do; to try to make love with a sexual man is the <u>last</u> thing you want to do!

'Sexual man takes what he wants.
Loving man gets what he wants,
Because woman freely gives it.'
by Sally Powell August 2003

Making Love is what man and woman were made for. To share a loving experience together is to become one in each others' bodies. As you do this together you evolve together. You remove the excitement and replace it with love. That way you continue to remain in what is known as the 'honeymoon period'. You continue to talk, continue to communicate and more importantly continue to remain 'in love'.

♥ Sally's Pages ♥

Well, where should I start? It became an issue (for me) as to whether I should write this page in the first place.

How My Life Has Changed

I made the suggestion to do it then did nothing more to actually get started. When this was brought to my attention I felt emotion rise in me...anger.

Upset by the feeling that it was being implied that I was not really bothered or didn't really care, this made it an emotion to face, to deal with rather than just saying, 'Oh, I will write it when I'm moved to!'

The point was, I saw if I only deal with things when I am 'moved to', I may always find an excuse not to do them. So this is how my life has changed...

At first I needed to be pushed to face all those years of hidden emotions, hurts and upsets, and get rid of them. But I also needed to learn from this and face things by myself and not wait for someone else to point them out. It's not easy. It can be very tough and at times I got to the point where I didn't want to do it any more because it hurt too much. But that is always the emotion talking, and as long as I saw this and didn't allow it to take control, I knew I would get through it.

You may ask then, 'Why bother if it hurts so much?' (Believe me, a question I have asked myself many times!) But the truth is, when the emotion is gone from the situation, if a similar situation arises again then I am able to see it and face it, and it's gone so quickly I feel little or no emotional pain. This way I am becoming free...free to enjoy, experience and fulfil my physical life with pleasure and love, not hurt and pain.

I now see the difference in other people who are run by their emotions, with the ups and downs and the constant problems; how

105

one person always seems to have things go wrong for them and those who are angry at the world and feel that everyone owes them. The important thing is that although I see this and recognise the way they are and feel, they do not affect me. I am only responsible for the way I feel and not how they feel, either about themselves or how they feel about me. I am responsible for how I treat them and my own behaviour towards them.

It has been tough for me. I've shed a lot of tears and felt a lot of physical pain as I struggle to rid myself of emotion. It has left me at times feeling totally exhausted and drained and completely empty, asking if I will be able to continue. But I do continue each time as all I want is love. Doesn't everyone?

Once the emotion at the time has been faced, a feeling of emptiness remains for a while, because I am empty: empty of emotion. But there is now plenty of space to be filled with good. This is a little uncomfortable at first but soon passes, and is replaced by the feeling of love, completeness and being whole again. This feeling makes it all worthwhile. As I said in 'Life with a Loving Man', love does not hurt. It's only the emotion that hurts.

The emotion wants to blame the man that is trying to get the emotion out. It raises its ugly head and blames him for anything he says and asks. But it's not his words that are to blame, it's the emotion which reacts to them. My emotions tell me that I am okay as I am and that I don't need to change or get rid of them. It even reacts to other people who tell me how much I've changed, and not all of them think for the better as I don't react to their emotions so much.

But change I have. My life is calmer, I feel more complete inside and my emotions no longer control my weight. I eat better and healthier and certainly have more energy. I am a vegetarian and no longer drink alcohol, and certainly feel better and more consciously aware that I have fewer toxins in my body.

But I am also aware emotion is still here and I still have a way to go. I hope one day to be completely free of it. It's amazing how the smallest thing can bring up such strength of emotion as to cause a reaction in sometimes such a horrible way. I do know that I don't want its pain, but until I can get rid of it all I just have to do my best to

106

face it when it comes and try not to let it blame anyone else but me. After all, I am the one who is responsible for it.

I do not know where the path of life will lead me, what trials and tricks it will play on me. I will probably have many more situations and events to face; some with Nick and some with others or on my own. But face them I must: it's the only way to set myself free. I have heard many people say that to get anywhere in life you have to stand alone...

Well, I am alone! There is only one being here. But if you have true love in your life, both the love given to you and the love you give to others, you may be alone in truth, but you are complete...I am complete! That is how my life has changed. I love and am loved. What more could any woman want...?

♥ Sally's Pages ♥

I have already talked about 'How My Life Has Changed', but it is interesting (to me anyway) how this has affected other people. (This page was written within a few months of first being with Nick.)

Why Can't They See What I See?

They seem to be focusing on what they see as the 'negatives' only. Even long-term friends pass comments like, 'Oh, you've changed!'

I think that as I remove the emotion in myself I detach from theirs, and this is the change they feel. The physical changes are irrelevant. The fact that I no longer wear makeup, became a vegetarian and stopped drinking alcohol seems to be what grabs their attention. But then they tell me that they wouldn't be able to do it or tell me about something they have recently changed in their life as if they are trying to bond with me or be like me or what I am doing.

People are so caught up in their emotions that they cannot imagine life without them and fear what it would be like. Everyone is so attached to 'objects', 'lifestyles' and 'image' that they fear letting go. They see in 'me' that I have and still am letting go. It's this that scares them and this is what they see when they say, 'Oh, you've changed.' The fact that I am calmer, more approachable seems to have escaped them on the frontal level, and they only see everything I do as a change not for the better.

Why can't they see that I am happier than I have ever been? I am with a man who shows me constant attention and affection; a man with whom I am happy to spend as much time as possible, who I put first and who puts me first. There is nothing more important than that.

Why can't they see?…Because they don't want to. They want to keep their pain and suffering because they feel comfortable with it, as I was for so long. They are happy with themselves; they 'know themselves', as they put it.

Everyone is looking for answers, looking for love and peace. The truth is there for everyone to see and it's so simple and it's free, you just need to open your eyes. Then everyone could see what I see: the good in people, the love and the peace; not just stress, pain and suffering, all because of emotion. Emotion is a heavy burden to bear. It's not easy to unload and I do not make light of the struggle, but it can be achieved in a relatively short time. The only requirement is to not want the pain any more.

Although I find that I am detaching myself from theirs and my own emotions, I still feel their love for me and mine for them. That will always be; but I have started this journey and do not wish to return. My only hope is that as time passes they will come to see the good as I do and join me here. Of course they will; after all, everything is a reflection of my being anyway – this I have already seen – so I have no fear that they will not. I will not lose them as they are a part of me. As I become less emotional I hope some of it will rub off on those around me, and they will begin to see what I see.

♥   Sally's Pages   ♥

I was listening to a song by Belinda Carlisle where she states 'They say in Heaven love comes first; we'll make heaven a place on earth'. These words have been ringing round my head for a couple of days, not only because it's a catchy tune but because that is exactly what I want.

Heaven on Earth

There are a lot of images conjured up when people try to describe what Heaven would be like...a place of beauty, bluebirds flying all over the place and everyone smiling at each other and being nice. Doesn't it sound perfect? Well let's just look at these words for a minute:

'A place of beauty': What is lovelier than a summer's day or a cold frosty morning, the first rain or the first flower?

'Bluebirds flying all over the place': Have you ever looked at all the different types of birds in the world; seen how beautiful they are with all their colours and delicate wings gliding on air?

'Everyone smiling at each other and being nice': Now this statement is why we do not have Heaven on earth. People smiling and being nice to each other is a rare thing indeed, and why is that? It's because they cannot see the beauty around them and just take for granted that it's there. After all, it was there yesterday so why shouldn't it be there tomorrow? People not only take their surroundings for granted but also the people around them. How often do you hear, when someone has lost a lover or close friend, how they wish they had told them how much they loved them before it was too late? In Heaven it's never too late because you tell each other all the time. You appreciate everything large or small.

We've been to a couple of weddings lately, and when I hear the bride and groom giving their vows I wonder if they have really listened to them or whether they were just thinking about the new

110

dress or shoes they've got on, and whether their hair looks right. Words are so easy to repeat, but it is the feelings that are important: how you feel about each other and how you show those feelings to each other. So many people seem to think that it's not 'cool' to show how they feel and that is really sad. I know I have done it myself and have been the receiver of this too; but to have someone show you affection as a lover or as a friend gives both of you a good feeling, and to make it happen you may need to start with yourself. You need to show how you feel; be happy to express your love for another and everything around you. Everyone likes to see a couple holding hands, lovingly teasing each other and, if they are honest, would like to share in it.

Sometimes, unfortunately, this can result in someone wanting to share in it too much and they will try to push themselves between you. In this instance you need to be on your guard and be honest with each other. Otherwise, if you try to hide that someone is 'being extra nice', when your partner finds out they may think you have got something to hide when it was not you at all! Honesty is important in any relationship. That way nothing and no one can do or say anything to surprise or upset you or come between you and your love. If not, you could find that you have created 'Hell on earth' where the love seems to have been lost or left you.

Thankfully we (Nick and I) have made 'Heaven a place on earth' and we fully intend to do everything we can to keep it; but believe me it's not really difficult once you learn to put love first...

Is Heaven just a dream in the clouds?
Or can we really experience 'Heaven on earth'?
I think we can.
We just need to look in the right place.

♥ Sally's Pages ♥

Can what you feel inside affect what happens around you? In my experience, yes it can.

As Within, So Without

I have heard this expression in the past so many times and just thought of it as some 'new age', sixties hippy saying, but as I get rid of more and more emotion within myself I see how the outside changes around me.

It has been said about me before that I have come across as confident, strong, hard and sometimes even a bit bossy, and I have to admit that I can see where the people who have made the comments are coming from; or should I say where I have come from! I used to feel that I had to be strong all the time and not appear weak, as this would be a sign of failure. I was all ready for a fight whenever I had to tell someone at work what I wanted them to do. So, I always got one...

I said before that my close, long-term friends have seen changes in me, and because they live some distance away and do not see me that often they are disturbed by them. The people I work with see me every day so the changes they have seen have been more gradual.

Now when I have to ask someone to do something, I do just that: I 'ask' and not give orders with a hidden undertone of expecting aggression back. At first people were not sure of me and were ready for me to revert back and were ready to defend themselves against me. But as the change in me becomes more constant and more a part of me without trying, they have come to accept the 'new' me.

I make sure that I take time before I act to take stock of what I say and the impression I want to give before going ahead with it, and over the time I have been practising this I have seen a big change in how others react to me. I no longer have to 'fight' to get things done.

112

People are happy to help; all they needed was for me to ask and not demand.

If they are having a 'bad day', I don't let it affect me as I am not the one they are angry with. So, by not taking anything they say personally and not reacting to them, I don't have to deal with their emotions. After a while they calm down and sort out whatever problem is bothering them and they come back and talk as if nothing has happened. But really nothing has, because as long as I don't accept their emotions when they are good or bad, they cannot bother me either way. By not letting them bother me, and by continuing to treat them in the same constant, unemotional manner, I no longer have anything to fight. This doesn't mean that I 'turn the other cheek' or back away when I feel that they are wrong. I am straight, firm and to the point if I have to be, but as long as I explain the reasons why I do what I do or say what I say, then they seem to accept it. I don't want to sound mushy to people, but it is true that what you give is what you get back: 'as within, so without'. There is no better expression for it.

Now I can sit back and watch other people deal with things the way I used to, and am thankful that it has been shown to me that there is another way. Why fight when you don't have to? I was only fighting against my own feelings anyway.

♥ Sally's Pages ♥

Having lived with a loving man for some months now, I was asked if I could go back to a sexual man. The answer is most definitely no…

Back to Sex?…No thank you!

I think any woman would tell you that the thought of having 'sex' is not what they really want; but the idea of 'Making Love' is wonderful. It doesn't have to be just imagination or a dream. The fairytale really can come true.

People may think that perhaps I am giving too much information here and I did wonder if I should really say anything or not, but the truth is all I have.

When answering the question above I said, 'No, thank you, as I have too much to lose!' I was then asked did that mean that I would be okay with the idea of the physical act, but just wouldn't do it for fear of losing something?

The thought of the physical act does send a shiver up my spine now, since it is (to me) aggressive and uncaring. Some people may argue that it's 'exciting', but excitement is short lived and a bit like a drug. It doesn't last long and the excitement fades so you need more and more to get the fix. This then turns into aggression if you don't get it.

In contrast, a person can Make Love all the time and just enjoy every moment; but there's no aggression, no wanting, just pure enjoyment. That is quite a key word, 'pure', because that is what real love-making is all about. I've managed to get the 'sex' and most of the emotion out of me, so why would I want to put it back? Go back to being with someone hard and aggressive? I don't think so. I used to suffer physically with problems many women can associate with – thrush, cystitis, feeling sore and aching – and the thought of having to do this 'act' every day…well, it just makes me shudder. It's no wonder women have so many what are termed as 'women's

114

problems'. The truth is, it's not women's problems at all, it's men that are the problem. They are the ones who inject their aggression and sexuality in to you.

Any doctor will tell you that it is good to have a healthy 'inside' and the only way to achieve this is not to abuse yourself or let anyone else abuse you. Making love is beautiful. It's soft, it's loving and caring. Your 'inside' needs as much love and attention as your heart does, and you know what it's like when that gets broken. So don't let your inside get broken. Only ever allow a loving man to enter you and make sure that he proves himself first. MAKE HIM WAIT 'TIL YOU ARE READY. That way you will be sure that he is with you for the right reason. There is nothing more precious that a woman can give than her body. Make him appreciate that. Don't be taken for granted; know that you are right. Woman is love and when you are love, living it daily means you feel fulfilled. Sex, unfortunately, rules the world. It would be so much nicer if it were replaced by love.

But sadly woman cannot do it alone. To be complete in love she needs a loving man to be with her and there are not many around. So as not to be negative, there are some, and when you find him you will experience (if you work together to get the emotion out of each other) a love worth waiting for. After all, love is what it's all about, isn't it?

♥ Sally's Pages ♥

Apart from looking for love, the one thing that I worried about <u>most</u> was my weight. How many magazines and companies claim to have the answer? – too many to mention – when the simple fact was, I had the answer in me all the time.

Weighing It All Up....

I have mentioned in my other pages about the weight I have lost and a lot of people now refer to me as 'The Disappearing Woman'. The truth is, I am, because I am striving to get rid of the emotion within me. This contributes greatly to my losing weight. I also have an advantage of having a loving man in my life and see now that I was overweight due to a lack of love.

I have since found that to lose weight is all about 'calories' and not much else. I exercised to tone up my muscles, but this did not help me to lose weight. I just simply watched what I ate and at the start checked the calories on everything. I was surprised when I noticed that the bottle of drink I take to work with me every day had so many calories in it. I make it up myself from squash and thought I was just drinking lots of water. When I looked at the bottle of squash and checked the calories, I found that I was having 400 per bottle each day, and that's without having any food. By buying the same flavour with 'no added sugar' I straight away reduced this to almost nothing.

Taking this simple example into context with everything else, I could then see how easily I could change what I ate, but I also needed to change the <u>way</u> I ate. I soon found I can have anything I like, as long as it's not all at once. I pace myself and if I have overindulged one day then I cut back the next. If I say I have only had a couple of chocolates from the box, I make sure that it is only a couple (two) and not four or five. I try to be honest with myself, and others. Otherwise, how will I ever hope to achieve anything of value

116

in my life, if I am prepared to lie about such a small thing as how many chocolates I have had?

I was surprised how easily the weight came off and in the end without even trying. It feels like I still eat 'loads', but it is all the right things at the right time. I've dropped from a UK size fourteen to a very easy size ten in only six months. I look and feel so much better and never have to worry 'does my bum look big in this?', because I know it doesn't.

There is what's often called 'comfort eating'. Food makes me feel good and I'm sure it does other people too (especially chocolate). When I used to be feeling down, depressed and unloved it was all too easy to reach for something nice to eat; something that would give me that 'feel good factor'. I imagine that this is the same feeling for any kind of compulsion, and when I really looked at it I could see that in giving into myself in this selfish way, I was not only affecting my weight but everything around me. That 'feel good factor' is only emotion wanting attention after all, and I was not only giving it what it wanted but I was feeding it physically as well. It was having a 'whale of a time', getting all the ups and downs, upsets and elations. This sounds like a yoyo and reminds me of the term 'yoyo dieting'.

I've managed to put a stop to it now; but have to be on my guard constantly as although this has to a certain extent become a way of life for me, emotion is very sneaky and can creep in just when least expected. I have seen myself falling into the trap of eating something just because I didn't get what I wanted somewhere else, when really it wasn't what 'I' wanted. It was what the emotion wanted. I found also that it is so easy to blame someone else for the way I was, because I didn't feel loved. I have heard it said about others: 'Since they got married she has let herself go.' I can understand that and I know now how important it is to put love first; not just for my partner but for myself as well, and this includes making an effort to look nice for each other. Why should I expect other people to like looking at me if even I do not like what I see; especially when I have the power to change it and it is self-inflicted due to a lack of love. By striving to look good for myself and my partner, and his acknowledging and appreciating me throughout, I have found the happiness I have

117

sought for so long, and the dress size. Just in case you think this sounds sexist, this applies to both, and Nick has taken up weight training again and looks wonderful. Now we look good for each other.

NB: Eighteen months have passed since I wrote the above and I have been a UK size eight for as long as I can remember now. I threw out all my baggy clothes which I had worn for so long to hide my shape and bought new, shapely, feminine clothes, the type of which I never thought I could wear. It's an absolute pleasure to be able to go to the shops and look for smart, fitted clothes (not revealing ones, since that goes into a whole different area) and I believe my overall enjoyment of life is demonstrated through how I look and what I wear.

118

♥ Sally's Pages ♥

It's been a while since I've written anything. Mainly because my life is so peaceful now that it ticks along very nicely. But a situation has happened recently that has drawn me to write about it.

Blaming Others

It's very easy (on the rare occasion it happens) to get upset about something someone says or does to me. The hardest part is looking at why it has hurt and upset me and it's much easier just to blame someone else for it, even if it's not their fault. Sometimes the only reason it hurts is because it reminds me of something that has happened to me in the past that I haven't dealt with or faced up to yet.

The situation happened whereby I received an email and felt like it was putting me down. (Unfortunately that is the trouble with emails; you can't actually see the person's facial expressions or hear the tone of their voice to really know what they mean and how they mean it.) I took the message the wrong way and got extremely emotional about it. At the time the emotion was so strong that I could not see the truth behind and blamed and accused the person who sent the email for making me feel that way. How dare they put me down? Who did they think they were? When in truth, what was a simple jest brought up the emotion of all the past times in a past relationship where I had been put down verbally. This reminds me of the expression 'Many a true word spoken in jest', and I suppose that expression could mean a few things. Either the person saying it is too irresponsible to tell me the truth nicely so they make a joke of it, or it's their way of expressing their own lack of confidence and it makes them feel better if they exert some kind of authority, in their mind, over me. It could also simply be, as was in this case, a light remark in humour reminding me of a past time.

By following Nick's teaching I first started to concentrate on my breathing, and this immediately started to calm me down. I was then able to become aware of where I was and how I was feeling. Before that, I was just in extreme emotional pain, crying and accusing. 'Typical woman' you might say, but 'typical emotion' I say. I was then able to see more clearly as to what it was that had actually upset me. Suddenly all those times when I had been put down came flooding back. It wasn't this person's fault at all. They didn't know what I had been through before and why should they? I've bottled it up for so long inside me that I can't even remember it sometimes. That is my trouble: burying stuff feels like the easiest and most convenient thing to do. Facing it is hard and painful and who wants that? When I did face it and see it for what it was, I was then able to deal with it. At last that bit of emotion has gone from within me. I am free of it, leaving a nice big hole for more love and consciousness to flood in. That certainly feels much nicer than a big hard lump of emotion.

Now if anyone says anything to me, I will be able to laugh and join in the joke and not feel that I am the joke. I was before, but only because I allowed myself to be. It feels quite empowering that no one will be able to have that kind of control over me again; no longer able to push the buttons to make me react. I am not here to be an outlet for their emotions. They can keep them and work on their own problem of lack of self-esteem; I have mine back.

♥ Sally's Pages ♥

Men: how to deal with them and how not to trust them when they are bearing such beautiful gifts? This is something that I have had to learn the hard way.

Diamonds May Impress, But Are They Real?

I know that many of my posts may come across as negative (though to me the learning has been very positive) and some people have commented that it appears that I have had a tough time and bad experiences in my life. Well yes, maybe I have, but I do believe that they are typical of a lot of people.

I found that I was easily impressed in my teenage years. Like most young people I was looking for excitement and experience, and travelled the world in my search for new and exciting things; so that's exactly what I got.

Being young and emotionally vulnerable, I thought that if a man gave me gifts, it meant that he liked me a lot, or even loved me. Experience now tells me this isn't true. To be truly loved by someone doesn't involve any gimmicks or symbols of any kind. It involves truth and honesty: two things that true love cannot live without.

Men can be very clever and very tricky. They know that women like 'shiny' (pretty or expensive) things and they see this as an easy way to 'get in'; and I let them, when I was younger. This was not because I was greedy and just wanted the presents (although I am aware that this can be the case in some people for various reasons), but I was young and inexperienced in mind games and wanted fulfilment in some form. By thinking that the gifts were a sign of 'love', I could not see when men were just being 'nice' to me to get what they wanted. If they were nice then they must have liked me, and that was enough. But men are much cleverer than that. They know just what to say and just what to do to get a reaction out of a woman. It's the men being 'nice' that I am more wary of now than the

121

ones just being basic and crude, because the latter are easier for me to see and recognise. My back instantly goes up when I come across this type of man, so I can avoid them; but with men being 'nice' I have had to learn to be even more on my guard to spot them, as I know now they are after the same thing as the crude, overtly sexual men and are just going about getting it in a more subtle way. I have learnt not to react when they try to be funny and even playful, when in the past I would have dropped my guard as the emotions are lulled into a false sense of security and tell me 'Oh, he is just being friendly'. This can be very dangerous and many women have been seduced by a smooth-talking man with the right lines when she is not loved enough in her life.

This sounds, as I am writing this, that I am unapproachable, cold and standoffish to men. I can see that, but this is not really the case, so I will try to explain what I mean. I have found in my experience that a man finds it difficult 'just to be friends' with me (perhaps most women find this), without wanting anything more. It is man's nature to be close to women and, if he sees one he is attracted to then why not try to be funny and playful, even if he knows that she is with someone else? Who knows, she may not be being treated properly by the other man and might be open to someone else?! So, as you see, I understand perfectly why he would do what he does and do not blame him for it. I am just aware of it and do not need to play the game now. I am lucky enough to be truly loved properly.

My point of writing this page is to say what you may already know all too well: just be aware of why men do what they do; of why a man you are not currently with may buy you beautiful gifts and why he may be nice to you. Of course he may be genuinely interested in you for the long term and not just seeing what he can get now. As I said, it is in man's nature to be close to women, so of course he will be nice and buy you things. The question is, how do you tell the difference between a man who is looking for a solid relationship to love and respect you, and one who is looking for a quick sexual fix? Besides the obvious and priceless advice of being cautious and making him wait until he proves himself, and not allowing his emotional cleverness to manipulate you into giving in before you are

122

satisfied that 'you are on the same page', I have found to date that to know the difference unfortunately only comes from experience with them and being aware of the signs. I now know what feels right to me and when I am being played. I have been caught out before when someone I thought was being 'nice' ended up stalking me when I later tried to say no, but that was an unfortunate extreme which can so easily happen to anyone if you attract the wrong person. Now, if I was to be approached by someone bearing 'gifts' (in whatever form, even a friendly smile), I am able to decide whether to accept them or not on my own terms, and not because I feel obligated or impressed. I can make a choice and be totally aware of why I make it, and can ensure it is not going to give the man any indication that there is a deeper meaning to it or lead him on in any way. The sexual drive in man needs to be given a wide berth and I have learnt, and am learning, how best to deal with the advances of a guy who thinks he has a chance and puts on the 'nice guy', 'innocent' approach. I don't fall for it any longer.

❤ Sally's Pages ❤

'I am this' is an expression I have heard many times, but what does this mean to me?

I notice, as Nick progresses with his work, that some of the emails he gets explain in detail the experiences that people have. They seem to go into lengthy descriptions with special terminology to describe how they feel and what they understand.

I Am This

(What this means to me)

This expression 'I am this' started to concern me because as I read more and more of the emails and letters Nick received, I started to feel inadequate because I didn't seem to understand what they meant or what they said.

I too have had great experiences during my time with Nick and have been lucky enough to have him with me all the time, to share them and explain to me what I was feeling and seeing. He thankfully understood my seemingly confused descriptions of what I was feeling and explained them to me, as he does with the letters and emails from others, in a way that made sense. But I remained concerned that I could not see for myself the explanations that people, both men and women, gave and the words they used. I continued to think and feel that I wasn't progressing as fast as I had hoped and felt that I still had a very long way to go.

Then one day, as I was reading a particularly in-depth email, it suddenly dawned on me. This particular person was trying to explain, understand and analyse everything, instead of just being it. Suddenly everything became clear to me. I don't need to understand what I am. I don't need to explain what I am and I don't need to analyse what I am. Just simply, 'I am this.'

I don't know if this is the difference between all men and women, but it seems to me to be very much the case. Men appear to need to search for the truth and answers, whereas women, in my experience, are simply the truth and love in existence. Once they get rid of all the questioning which gets in the way and settle into the being of it, the truth is simply 'I am this'.

Now when I read the letters and emails and accompany Nick on his talks, I understand everything perfectly without actually understanding anything at all. If someone asks me a question, I try to explain as best I can, but have to tell them that 'I am this', and I just live what I am and do not feel the need to explain or even justify why. It's probably not very helpful to those who are looking for answers, but I have found that when Nick is talking to a couple, the woman usually understands me perfectly as she feels the same way: there is no need to understand, analyse and question. Just simply sit back, relax and love, in the feeling 'I am this': truth and love in existence.

♥ Sally's Pages ♥

'For men it is quick, easy and essential for reproduction. For women, it is slow, difficult and purely for pleasure.'
(Source: 'The story of Ohh!', *Guardian*, 28 April 2004)

The above piece is the opening line from an article looking at the differences of orgasm in men and women.

The Difference Between Making Love and Sex

Nick has written many pages on the difference between love and sex. I thought it would be a good idea to write from a woman's point of view, after reading a very interesting article all about the differences between a man's orgasm and a woman's, taken from the book *The Intimate History of the Orgasm* by Jonathan Margolis.

The article provided a lot of information from all different perspectives, from the scientific physical side to the emotional, and the theories detailed certainly got me thinking. All the theories and ideas in the article seemed either to be from a man's viewpoint or from feminists (some of whom can appear to be quite masculine in the sense of male aggression and sexuality; not all, but some) so I would like to give my views as to what these ideas are to me and my experience of the 'climax' of love-making as opposed to sex.

I think many would agree that generally women fall in love first and lust second, whereas men are prone to fall in lust first and then struggle with the love bit. This is not through any fault. Men are just further removed from the state of love or consciousness due to their sexual predatory nature, and find it harder to learn to find the sensitivity again. This innate openness and awareness is demonstrated by what we call 'women's intuition', where women are famous for picking up on subtle signals, consciously or otherwise, to which men seem oblivious. Thankfully I am with a man who is

126

Enlightened and in the state of love all the time, so he can understand my needs and emotions as and when they arise.

It seems, according to the article, that most people think a woman can only orgasm through manual physical stimulation of the clitoris and apparently, as described by scientist Stephen Jay Gould, this part of the female body is just a version of the man's penis anyway, which is why she will get the same feelings as him in that place. This may be so, but what about all those women who claim to have multiple orgasms? Are they faking it?

I think man is all about basic sensations (and that is not a judgement on my part, or indeed any kind of put down; it is just an observation). He can be touched by anyone or any-'thing' and his body will automatically react without him having to do, or imagine, anything. For me, I do not get the same kind of feelings. I do not have the need to be touched by anyone or any-'thing' else, other than by my partner in our loving relationship.

For me it is all about being in a loving relationship, sharing each other's bodies and experiences to become more complete and whole. I do not feel the 'need' to have an orgasm through physical stimulation as seems popular. That's not to say I don't enjoy holding each other as loving couples do, but that is all it is and there is no need for me to go into imagination or to 'get in the mood', as also seems popular. What is important is the total pleasurable experience of love-making. I don't believe I have ever had an orgasm through sexual intercourse as commonly understood, which actually agrees with the article where they state this is the experience of most women. It's hard for me to remember now exactly, as I have moved so far away from that. My only release at that time (in previous relationships) was through the physical stimulation, as during intercourse I knew deep down that I wasn't being loved. I understand when some women say how wonderful manually stimulated orgasms are, when really I don't think they have been shown another way. I hadn't before learning about love.

Orgasm through physical stimulation, in my previous experience, took quite a while to build up and then there was a sudden burst of sensation which disappeared quite quickly. It then left me with a feeling of self-loathing and the feeling that it was wrong. This may have been partially due to my upbringing, but I think more because I knew that the next step was sex and I knew I wouldn't have any feelings there, other than knowing he was just enjoying himself inside me. The manual orgasm was his payment to me for his orgasm inside me afterwards. It was a compromise and trade-off.

Now, when climaxing through making love, it is what I call wonderful every time in a way I only ever imagined and never really thought was possible. Reading all the details in the article as to what happens to the body, and how your toes curl and your heart pumps faster and your body sweats, explains all the physical sides but doesn't really explain how I feel at that moment. To me the sensation starts at the very beginning and gradually builds to completion at the same time as my partner, each and every time. I have a tingling sensation all over my body with a feeling of total openness and giving; which is how I think a woman is, naturally open and giving. But this only happens for me because my partner is not taking for himself, but giving himself totally to me. Thus we are giving and receiving each other.

The article also states that a man needs to orgasm in order to reproduce whereas a female does not. This appears to be an unquestionable fact but it also goes on to say that for women it appears to be just a pleasurable experience. To me it is far more than this. It is the essence she feels when she knows that her man loves her and is showing her that he does. I think therefore there are two different types of orgasm. One is reached through sexual excitement, which everyone knows about, and one through making love, which is elusive and rare.

The article says an orgasm achieved through manual stimulation is more 'intense' than in sexual intercourse, but in my experience this was only because I knew it was all I was going to receive. Now an orgasm through making love is always intense because it is a joining together, giving each other total commitment and pleasure, consciously, rather than through imagination and excitement.

128

I can hear all the voices saying, 'Huh, love-making is just another name for sex.' Well the act may be the same in some cases, but the intention and the experience are very different in my experience. I also believe that men have taught women to like physical stimulation as an alternative to love-making, so they do not have to put any effort in to making sure that she gets the love she deserves.

I believe my own view also explains why it is said 'men place more importance on the orgasm itself and women place more importance on the relationship'. They have different needs. Men are looking for women to satisfy their basic sexual need, whereas I am looking for someone to love me properly (which is my basic need). If only men could realise that if they loved me (woman) properly, complete and whole, they would get everything they wish for. In my experience that is certainly the case.

The article I refer to may not be everyone's view, but it gave rise to this piece and is just my view on how it relates to my own experiences.

♥ Sally's Pages ♥

Nick and I have been together now for three years and it is some time since I wrote anything about us. I have called this 'Growing Younger' because that's how I feel.

Growing Younger

I have described my journey through my other pieces as I passed through each new phase. Maybe phase isn't the right word as that implies to me that it's something not permanent. But I feel that my life is more permanent now than it has ever been, as I have become each of those phases and not just passed through them.

As I have learnt to take control of my emotions, getting rid of most of them (experienced as being steadier and having fewer reactions to situations), I am freer and more open to new things. Having lost the weight and being honest about what I eat, I have kept it off. I'm now not worried about what people see and am more confident in the way I look. However, I am also well aware of how I dress and understand how not to put myself into a situation that I do not want. It's one thing to be pleased with how I look, but it would be quite another to flaunt it.

Facially I have also changed. I no longer have the heavy stressed look that I used to try to cover with makeup. My face is fresher, lighter and even has fewer lines! So no more wasting money on magic creams for me. I have found my answer to the fountain of youth: it's a good, clean, healthy, loving relationship with a loving man-

A simple example of the change: We recently had a lovely two-week holiday on the island of Majorca where Nick, after two years of trying, taught me to snorkel. It may sound petty and silly to all of you who can do this, but I had a real fear of not just trying it but also looking stupid for trying. My reasoning in myself was that I was too old to do that sort of thing, but it went deeper than that. I also for the first time went to a water park. That was my idea and when Nick asked me why I was so insistent on going (not that he minded at all as he likes them) I said it was because I felt that I am now able to enjoy my life and try new things, as I know that he will support and encourage me and not put me down or humiliate me.

It has made such a difference to my life. I would sometimes put other people down if they tried anything, not because I wanted to be mean but to cover up for my own inadequacies, as I thought I had some. I didn't really. I just lacked confidence and this did result in me being mean to others. That has stopped now and I am much more understanding of how people feel and how what I say affects them.

There is an age gap of fourteen years between myself and Nick, he being the younger, and I am well aware that some people think that's why I feel so young. This may well be a contributing factor, but for me it's love that is the answer; and love that lasts.

Because of the caring, affectionate and attentive way in which he treats me, I know that I am being loved totally and it is that which is putting a spring in my step. I have heard many people talk about the 'honeymoon' period and how a relationship then moves out of that and into an 'understanding' of each other. I agree with the understanding part, but have to disagree with moving out of the honeymoon part. For me it is still here. After three years I still get a spark light up inside me every time I see him, even if it's an hour or a few minutes after we last saw each other.

Every time we are together I want to hold and caress him and I know he feels the same way. A lot of my friends tell me about how they need space from their partners, some of them having not been together very long, but Nick and I are happy to be together all the time. Life and work dictates that sometimes we are not able to, but we know that the idea that spending too much time together can spoil a relationship can be the case, but it does not have to be that way.

So, to me the answer to staying young is simply to find a man who knows how to love you. I did.

Sally Powell

Revelations

The contents of this next section even surprised me as I wrote them at the time. The descriptions sometimes question and perhaps contradict not just the words of others but even what I have said previously. As self-knowledge or God-Realisation deepens, new ways of explaining and perceiving what is can occur. None of the earlier pieces have been removed as all are the truth in the points they attempt to portray. However, these writings are likely to undermine a lot of what is already 'out there', as well as what is in here.

Nick Roach

I had always heard and accepted that God was the ultimate; that God was the supreme highest state and the absolute beginning of the beginning...that is, of course, if you accept God exists at all.

As the experience here, often called 'God Realisation', deepens, new knowledge and insights are occurring which call into question even my own accepted views.

Is God the Ultimate?

As with many of these insights, they are obvious once they are pointed out:

I am going to say that 'God', as we give meaning to the name, is not the ultimate, and I will explain why. However, God is certainly the ultimate with regards to what we can experience here, and I shall explain this too.

Let's have a look at what 'God' means to us, because in the end it is just a word with a meaning attached, and that will help us to answer the question.

'God', we say, is the creator of all things. God is omnipotent and knows all. There is nowhere that God is not, and it is said that to realise 'God' is to realise oneness with the universe.

However, can you see the problem with the above? If God is the creator of all things, then God is the cause of the separation. What we call 'God' is the original point where it all began, where the need to experience first emerged from the oneness of nothing, and thus all else came into existence. Therefore God is NOT the ultimate. God is the beginning of separation and the beginning of everything. The ultimate is what was before anything emerged; even before the need for anything emerged; even before God. Can you see this?

It is pretty bold stuff and I don't think it has ever been said before, but when we worship God, we are actually worshipping the essence that needed to exist in the first place; the essence that needed to experience the pain and the wonder of being separate,

135

and of gaining and losing, hoping and trying, of wanting and fearing. God is the one who wanted this and created all this, thus we pray to him for help when it is all too much. There is no point in praying to the oneness, as it is just what is supporting it all without need for anything. And how could you pray to the oneness anyway? There is nothing to pray to, which is why we must pray to God, which is at least something, even if it is nothing as a specific object; because God is every object. God is creation as the 'oneness' is beyond creation. I use the word oneness but even this is, of course, incorrect as it implies some alternative. The word is correct here as we (you) are the alternative, but in truth there is nothing but oneness.

So, continue to look for God if you wish. If you are fortunate you will have glimpses that God is everywhere, in all the birds and trees and all around you, and maybe even that you are God. But don't be fooled into thinking that is the ultimate, because any-thing is still something, and some 'thing' is not the ultimate. The ultimate is even beyond the knowing of anything; so while you know anything, while there is something to be known and someone to know it, this is clearly not the ultimate. The ultimate is beyond all knowledge, all knowing and all experience; even beyond what we call 'God', the creator of separation.

We have been taught of the eternal battle between God and the Devil; of how God fights to maintain paradise but the Devil, even the Devil within us, is spoiling all that is good and seducing the weak to follow him. These days we are moving away from the idea of the Devil as an external force, but there still remains the belief in a God of some sort and the question 'Why does God allow this?'.

What if I was to say that as far as I can see God and the Devil are the same thing? This may well stir a few things in people, but I ask you to read the following and have a look at what is written, restricting any emotion from reacting if any rises in you, if you can.

Is God the Devil?

Is this a stupid question? Everyone knows the Devil, if anything, is opposite to God and opposing God; that the Devil is the bad force that causes all suffering and God is the good force that supports us in our hour of need. When things are wonderful we can often be heard to shout 'Thank you, God!' and when times are tough 'Help me, God'.

Well, if you read the earlier page 'Is God the Ultimate?' you may have understood that God is the essence or energy that needs to exist; that God is the creator of all separation and thus the cause of all pain and suffering. We pray to God to make us complete in our hour of need, not giving a thought to any consequences that may result to others. 'God, help me win', we all pray. 'God, give me what they've got'...'God give me everything'! The fact that for us to win means another must lose is of no consequence to us at the time. We then blame God when all goes wrong and we don't get what we want. We ask 'Why, God...why?' and have comforting sayings such as 'God works in mysterious ways'. We need such sayings now, because we are beginning to see that God is responsible for all that happens, both the good and the apparent bad. Whether we win or lose are both down to this 'being' we call God, but if this is the case, then why does this 'being' seem to like to win or lose equally?

The answer is: because it has created this existence to experience being separate and this includes losing as much as winning. In fact one could say, it often prefers losing having had the hope of winning, more than winning itself, as to lose after investing all the emotional effort can generate more feeling and more sensations than winning; which is what this game is all about. This wonderful creation that God has provided is a playground for feeling. You feel good one day and down the next, often with no understanding of why you feel that way; but it doesn't matter: the fact is, you feel.

I had always believed, or accepted without question, that when it came to spiritual matters, the ultimate is God. Likewise, the need for experience, the need to be separate, could be said to be the Devil, as it is this part that separated from the whole and created this world of opposites and suffering. However, as we have seen, the fact that God created the world, created separation, means it was not the Devil after all. Or if it was, it is not something separate from God but an aspect of God's own being.

Can you see this? Can you see how this means that the very thing we worship is the same thing that we fear? In fact, how could it be any other way, when we consider that we say God is the ultimate and is in everything and omnipotent? The fact that we do say he is omnipotent means he must be in the Devil too; mustn't he? It is God which was the original force that created this existence, not the Devil, and it is the same force that drives it and governs all that happens here. It is this force which drives us to experience, to want, to hope, to fear, to hate, to love and to kill. It is the one force driving all existence and it is what we return to when we realise 'God'.

To realise 'God', in the sense of Enlightenment or Self-Realisation, is not to realise 'good' as opposed to 'bad'. In this state there are no opposites as all is one. There is only what is and what is, is perfect, as there is no 'bad'. Each moment provides exactly what is needed here to satisfy the need to experience, whether the mind labels it as good or bad. Neither matters as both satisfy the

138

same need: the need to be. The 'ultimate' cannot be experienced here as there is nothing to experience there, and when it occurs it is because there is no need left to experience or be anything; thus nothing to know or be known. Until then we continue to live the drama as it is played out in our lives.

So, God and the Devil are both opposite ideas of the same force. Neither one is the truth as you, the essence you can feel now, are both (the one and only). There is only the ultimate which cannot be known and the need for experience being satisfied in its own world. There is no God as a separate creator of all that is good, and no Devil as a destroyer of good. Both are the same need to experience which you are living now, until both disappear.

The Bible always talks of God being 'He' and even of God making man in his own image. More recently, in these days of equal rights for women, many now say God is neither male nor female and most people question whether God exists at all. So, can we really know whether God is male or female?

Is God Really Male?

The answer is: 'Yes, we can know the answer, as we look deeper into what God is and what the male and female energies are.'

If you have read the earlier pages in this section, you will have seen that I say God is the original point of separation, the first movement or need to experience which then created all else. So, we have two 'areas' to speak of:

      1) The 'ultimate' or oneness where there is no-thing;

      2) 'God', which is the original energetic separation from the whole, which then creates all else.

If we have a look at the differences between men and women here, we may start to see the truth behind the two apparent opposites:

Woman conceives life here, with a piece from the man, and carries the embryo in her own body, feeding and protecting it before giving birth. Once the baby is born she continues to feed the young from her own body, holding it close and giving to it totally and selflessly. The female energies are the giver of life; the source and sustaining force behind all that is experienced. We even give nature the title 'Mother Nature' or Mother Earth', as we acknowledge the female essence in the beauty and grace of what is provided naturally. On a human level, woman generally looks to be loved. She is not usually as interested in what we term 'man's world', of creating bigger and faster nuclear warheads, spaceships and technological advancements and so on. She is not out to change the world, to control, to destroy, nor interested in many of the characteristics man

140

(in general) has done and is doing. Woman may look to produce children and be with them, but in the first place she looks to be loved and put first by her man. (I know these are huge generalisations, but please bear with me.)

Man is the achiever (at the risk of going further into old stereotypes). Man is the one with the testosterone through his body. He is the one who looks to fight, to achieve, to go higher, faster and bigger; to prove himself and put his mark on the world. Man knows, at some deep level inside him, that his woman wants to be loved and put first, but he just can't do it. Football, earning money, driving cars, drinking, gambling or generally doing as he pleases so he does not feel controlled are a small sample of what man indulges in, instead of loving the woman he is with and putting her first. And yet he is obsessed with sex, with the female form, as it is well known. This world is built on man's lack of love and consciousness, and his drive for greater stimulation and excitement, and many everyday products are linked in some way to sex when being advertised for sale. He can barely help but imagine being closer to any woman he finds remotely attractive, always believing he is (or wishing he was) the world's greatest lover; as if he knows that his true purpose is to love…and yet he just can't do it. His need for more and more experience always drives him to look for what's next beyond the one he is with and what he is doing at any given moment.

And what is next? Just more separation in the quest for experience. In relationships it is the going from the woman he is with to another woman, whom he also quickly takes for granted then to look for another or for some other way to alleviate his need for more and more and more.

Can you see here which of the two original points are either male or female? Can you see that the female, as we experience it here, is representative of the ultimate oneness which gives all and wants for nothing other than to be put first by the male? And the male is representative of God, the point of separation from the ultimate, from the female, looking for more and more experience and pleasing himself, while knowing he is separate and wanting to get back to her. And yet he can't stay with her for long, as he has too much else to do.

Man sees the female form here in existence and senses the energy within her which he has left, and it is his deepest desire to return there. Yet his attachment to his playground of satisfying his own feelings is too strong to give up completely at this time. Woman also feels the separation from him, often longing for the male energies to return to her and for him to put her first above all else; loving her and adoring her as if nothing else mattered. Hence you have the basic difference between the sexes: Man wants sex (excitement) and woman wants love (union). God (in the sense of attachment to existence and the male energies) wants to remain separate and enjoy playing and experiencing what he has created, while woman, the ultimate, waits for him to come home to her.

This representational model can be taken further still, when you consider that science tells us that all human foetuses start off as female, with only the 'X' chromosome. It is only with the addition of the 'Y' chromosome that the male qualities begin to evolve within the female foetus, inside the body of the mother where all is originally conceived. So, as you can see, God is indeed male, but he came out of the female. She is his home, his love and his very being. She is the ultimate, waiting for him to return home when he has had enough of 'playing outside'.

142

I have said I followed Barry Long's teaching for many years and it was through his teaching that I came to the realisations I have had. They say 'the Master' must stand alone, and it has been interesting seeing how I have developed (or it has developed in me) my own style and outlook, which is different in some areas from those of Barry.

That is why this page is in this section. It's a revelation to me actually to contradict something Barry said. That is not to say he is wrong, since these insights are a matter of perspective, but this is mine...

The End of the World?

I will post this as I received and answered the question:

Q)   Nick, I followed Barry Long's teaching for many years and in one of his tapes he talks in some detail about the end of the world. I notice you do not talk about this; in fact many teachers don't. Why is this?

A)   Thank you for your question. It is a popular idea that all Enlightened people will have the same knowledge and indeed will even act in the same way. This is not the case.

What happens is simply the person has seen through the illusion of the separate forms to see the space experienced within is the same space creating everything (and this remains with them as a living experience and is not a fleeting glimpse or insight). From here the experience may be interpreted, and indeed explained, in many different ways, according to the person describing it and who they are talking to etc.

With regards to your question, once a person is in the experience of 'being at one' (or whatever you wish to call it), the mind can then make reasonable observations, and even assumptions and predictions, as to what is and what is likely to occur, should things continue. Hence you get examples of teachers such as Barry Long making predictions as to the end of the world. Barry was my own teacher and it was through following his teaching to the letter that I came to where I am now. It is therefore interesting to me that the knowledge of the end of the world has not come to me in the same way as he described it.

I cannot speak for Barry, but I can understand how a person in the 'Enlightened state' could see how evolution could be moving towards a time when all do indeed become Enlightened: when the continuation of the dream has been going on long enough, has been 'around' enough times, that the Enlightened state does not just occur in the individual but in all apparent individuals at that time who are 'ready' to make the transition. However, I see things differently...

To me, this dream or existence is here for the individual to enjoy being separate until s/he no longer needs or wishes to be. Then the dream ends. Until it ends, the dream allows for the idea (if not the reality) of the continuation of itself and for the belief in the illusion to be supported by 'evidence'. This evidence includes not just the many different people all apparently looking for Enlightenment (let's say) but also the fact they are all on different levels of self-awareness within 'their own' dreams. The world as a whole provides places for great misery, great suffering, great beauty and all levels in between. There is a definite need for all these things. Why? Because the spirit, where it is very 'young' in the dream sense, still needs to experience gross separation, becoming finer with each form ('incarnation' if you like) until eventually going within itself where it began and all is complete. Removing the circumstances offering this 'service' would remove the possibility for a new dream(er) to enjoy the separation to the extremes that is required (in order for it to eventually 'wake up'), since everyone would already be 'awake' or Enlightened...

How does the above relate to Barry Long's teaching of the end of the world, if you are not familiar with it? Well, were the world to end in the way Barry taught (that the world is to be burnt out of all those who are ready, resulting in everybody remaining afterwards being Enlightened) how would that serve the 'new' dream(ers) coming through? Of course it wouldn't. There would be no 'young dreamers' or people living in ignorance early on in their journey, as

144

there would only be Enlightened persons. Thus this would be the end of the continuation of the dream.

If you take it, as many teachings do (and particularly the older ones), that this dream, or illusion, or Maya should indeed be ended 'asap' as it is not real, then one can understand how this view of the end of the world would seem a logical conclusion to the cycle of lifetimes: the view that everyone who is not Enlightened and 'awake' should be. However, for me, I do not see this dream as a bad place. I do not wish for it to end, or for me or for anyone else to wake up any quicker or any more than they do, until it is time. I am not out to deny those 'younger' souls (for want of a better term) their right to enjoy the dream and work their way up to conclusion; for it to begin again later anyway (chances are). For me, there is nothing wrong with the dream. There is nothing wrong with being asleep and there is nothing wrong with being wherever you are, or seem to be, along the way to 'waking up'. This dream is to be enjoyed, whatever stage you are at. No judgement here. No 'good or bad'. Just life living.

So, this is why I do not talk of 'the end of the world'. It will end as a complete entity for the individual who 'wakes up' and no longer needs the forms; but the dream itself encompasses all levels and therefore I do not see a need for it to end in the sense of 'forcing' a number to 'wake up' and destroying the rest, as Barry (and perhaps others) described.

I hope this is okay for you? You may have been looking forward to the end of the world, as a 'get out', but the true end of your own suffering is the space within you, where you are complete. Find this and you are responsible. Longing for the world to end outside of you and make everyone Enlightened, to make your life easier as some people do, is not being responsible.

On a practical note and to make the point further, the world provides all possibilities here for experience. Un-Enlightened people watch the news and enjoy all the usual goings on, but so do many Enlightened people. It is not unheard of for an Enlightened person to read the papers and watch the news, and indeed to get involved in trying to make things better here. Why? Because it is right for them that they do. If the world was to end as some teach, these experiences would be denied to all who could benefit from being involved with them, or simply from being touched by them. This place is a place of separation and opposites, which includes gross pain and suffering and atrocities and ugliness, as well as all the beauty we see here. Therefore I don't see the world ending as a whole, in the way you ask. There were many years when I too longed for it, or at least for an end to the pain in me, but I found it, and the world did not need to end, as you can see, as we are both still here. Can you find the end of the pain within you while the world is still here? It can be done.

This is another revelation for me because it undermines what I was taught and therefore was more than a little strange as I began to see it. Many teachers imply, even if they don't announce categorically, that you should be Enlightened to be your true self. Below is my own view on this now...

Your Natural State!?

The very first cassette I listened to by my teacher was to become my favourite throughout my years of following the teaching and included his stating strongly: 'To be Enlightened is to be an ordinary man or woman, and it is every man and woman's RIGHT to be an ordinary man or woman!' So that was my 'benchmark'. Everyone would/should be Enlightened, if only they were natural or ordinary.

It was not until it occurred here, many years after first hearing the words and having heard them to the point of almost knowing the entire cassette 'off by heart', that I began to see that there is another possibility here. This was the possibility that perhaps it is also every man and woman's right NOT to be Enlightened, as much as to be Enlightened.

Do you get this? Do you see that there is actually a great judgement in stating that to be 'ordinary' is to be Enlightened and it is your RIGHT to be Enlightened?

I must say, I do not write these pages to take anything away from Barry Long whose great teaching taught me everything and resulted in me being able to write this. I write because it is new. It is my own teaching and a part of me finding my own approach and style, and perhaps most importantly I wish to remove any judgement people have about this state. I do not say it is better to be Enlightened! It's simply the natural progression of the individual from being asleep, 'day-dreaming' (being lost in the illusion), to beginning to wake up and see it for what it is. No one bit is better than another, for one part must follow the other.

The cassette also included Barry 'invoking all the forces of nature to take anything from him, be it an arm or whatever, if it would make him more pure'. So, in Barry's Enlightened state, the urge to become purer was so strong that he would invite this, even if it meant losing all else. This at first may (and it did to me) sound like a complete non-attachment to anything and was quite impressive, but you may see it is actually a strong attachment to the experience, or idea, of becoming purer, whether real or imagined.

I have looked at this and asked myself a little while ago, 'Do I want to invoke all the forces of nature to take anything from me if it would make me more pure, be it my health, my partner, my job, my money, my house, my gorgeous little dog, in fact anything I love to allow me to tell myself it is making me purer?', and the answer is 'No!'. I then had to look at why this was, and I saw it was not because I can't bear to lose these things, but because I have no need for anything to change, until it does. If it is right for me to lose something I love, so be it. No complaints here. But I am not going to go out of my way to invite something I love to be taken from me, just so I can tell myself, or have an experience, that I am becoming purer because of it.

Seeing this is actually a big thing for me, since it does mean questioning my own Master (of many years). Some may say I should not write this for the above reason, while others have criticised me in the past for my teaching being too much like Barry's, so either way people are going to be disturbed, but on with the page...

If you really believe that to be Enlightened is to be your natural state, I would like to suggest to you that very little changes. Actually you just see you are dreaming all this; but be under no illusion please that you ARE still dreaming. The dream does not end just because you become Enlightened (or I would not be writing this). All that happens is that you know it's a dream, and walk around all the time knowing it, but it does not end at that point.

Once all need for the dream has been satisfied, I have said elsewhere that the dream ends, but is that really to be your natural or ordinary state? In truth, we don't know! All we 'think' we know of that state is that there is (or will be) nothing left to know anything, since

148

all need of anything has been satisfied. I am not in a hurry to get there, but I do also not *want* to remain here. I am very content now whatever happens, exist or not.

Also, many of the teachers of this view (who believe that this illusion or dream should be ended as fast as possible as it is not real) also teach that this life is actually perfect: that all is as it should be and everything happens for a reason! I have to ask here, surely therefore if everything is perfect and always has been, then it is perfect NOT to be Enlightened too; isn't it?

The point of this page was really just for me to question the common views, which I too held and many Enlightened people seem to agree with, while expressing a major difference in perspective from my own teacher to whom I am still grateful for all he gave. He did say that after he was gone another would have to come to say things clearer than he could. I am not claiming that he was talking specifically about me, but simply that things must move on. That is what is happening here.

The idea for this page has kept recurring in me for a number of weeks now. It relates to the increasing numbers of people proclaiming to the world that they are Enlightened, having had the insight that there's nobody and nothing here or some other fleeting insight. Some of these are quite famous while others are new to the scene and write to me, inviting me to read their work. Either way, I thought it a good time to write a page about, what I am calling...

Phoney Enlightenment

What does this mean, and how can any Enlightenment be phoney?

Of course it can't be phoney, if indeed it is Enlightenment. The trouble is, until a person is actually Enlightened, they don't know what it is. They therefore look around at who else is calling themselves Enlightened and how they describe it, and decide 'Hey, that description is close to what I have experienced, so I must be Enlightened!'. I am referring to all those who announce they are Enlightened having had the insight 'There is nobody here, there is nothing here and this is nothing happening to nobody!', or even that they have briefly seen that they are 'one' with everything and are a part of God.

In case you are wondering why this page is a 'revelation', it is because on seeing that some of these chappies were quite well known and widely accepted as being authorities on the subject, I overlooked the many contradictions with my own experience, preferring instead to tell myself they were simply explaining it in a different way.

So, I brushed off the above repeated philosophy, that there is no one to be Enlightened and no one and nothing here. I also skimmed over when one of these 'teachers' announced when I was with him 'These Enlightened teachers don't know there is no one to be Enlightened and no one to teach!'. I also let it go when I introduced myself to him as one of these teachers and he told me 'It's confusing
150

to people!' (but he did say it with a smile). And with regards to the myriads on the forums who were announcing the same ridiculous (to me) statements, I would take it that these people had just got the idea and were repeating what they had understood (which was often the case).

The final dawning for me was when I received two emails within a couple of weeks from different people, both claiming to be Enlightened having seen the above, or something similar, in an experience. When I 'tested' one who had invited me to visit his own website, which he had set up to teach others this, by asking about his experience and insight in relation to my own, after a couple of emails he replied finally that I was mad, saying '...*I guess I totally misunderstood you...Must be lonely being the only individual in the universe! And here you are creating "me" telling you that I am "one" with the vast "Cosmos"...Sorry for the misunderstanding...but now that I take you literally...it seems absurd to me....This is the end of the conversation.*'

So, that was the turning point. I had been a little seduced by people who were 'around' before me, who some may regard as almost famous, or at least established and quite respected. Who was I, a young lad (relatively speaking) and new to the scene, to question these authorities? Well here, on the pages in this section, I am questioning a lot of things which I had previously taken on faith. Why should this be any different? Below I will see if I can explain to you why these chappies are 'phoney', whether they are aware of it or not, so you will understand totally how obvious it all is.

What we are really looking at here is why we (myself included) should accept my experience of Enlightenment as being genuine and the others as being false? One, if not both descriptions, must be wrong. They are opposite or at least very different and are not compatible, so who should you believe?

Well, let's begin by saying any belief is not the truth. Even if the teaching you accept is from a person speaking the truth, until you experience it for yourself, it is just words 'pointing the way'. So, what I am going to do here is explain very clearly what the options are and

151

you can make up your own mind, while being aware you still need to 'become it' to truly know, and not just believe.

The situation: I state I am Enlightened. I say it is the experience and not just a knowing, knowledge or insight, and not just a flash or feeling that comes and goes, of everything 'I' (meaning 'you') experience being within my own intelligence; that all that is here is 'my' own creation and I am responsible for everything that happens. I am indeed 'God Realised' as I have realised (real-ised = to make real) that 'I' am 'God' (making no statements as to what either of these is, but they make up the experience of 'I' and all else).

In contrast, these other teachers who claim to be Enlightened (or say they are not as no one is, while claiming to be in the experience to know this) say either 'all is one' and that they are a part of this great being and are one with the 'cosmos', or they say they have seen there is nobody here, nothing here, no one to be or to know anything and certainly no one to be Enlightened.

To answer this dilemma I would like to take this away from me and back to the original teachings from Eastern religions and philosophies. This way you do not need to accept my word for anything and can look at a third point of view which may be an established authority.

Many who dispute what Enlightenment is do accept the Buddha (the word itself meaning Enlightened One) as being Enlightened. You may recall the teachings direct the individual to go within and realise their true self, often called 'Self-realisation'.

So, here is a small reminder of what the Buddha is reported to have taught:
'Only within our own body can bondage and suffering be found, and only here can we find true liberation.'
'Within this fathom-long body is found all the teachings, is found suffering, the cause and the end of suffering.'
'To find a Buddha, you have to see your own nature. Whoever sees his own nature is a Buddha.'
When asked if he was special, he is recorded to have said simply '...I am awake.'

152

'You are the light, you are the refuge, there is no place to take shelter but yourself.' (Inscription over the Buddha's ashes)

Also, many may be familiar with the Hindu spiritual text the Bhagavad-Gita, which contains the teachings of Krishna and talks at length about the aim of realising the Supreme Personality which exists within every living thing:

'I am the Supersoul, O Arjuna, seated in the hearts of all living entities.'

'I am the beginning, the middle and the end of all beings.'

'Just fix your mind upon Me, the Supreme Personality of Godhead, and engage all your intelligence in Me.'

'The Supersoul is the original source of all senses, yet He is without senses.'

'Although the Supersoul appears to be divided among all beings, He is never divided. He is situated as one.'

'I am seated in everyone's heart.'

'The Supreme Lord is situated in everyone's heart.'

'A true yogi observes Me in all beings and also sees every being in Me.'

'Indeed, the self-realised person sees Me, the same Supreme Lord, everywhere.'

And even the Bible, whether true stories of a man called Jesus or revamped pagan stories, describes one God which is omnipotent and in all things, and teaches:

'I and the Father are one.'

'I am the way, and the truth, and the life; no one comes to the Father, but through Me.'

'Be still and know that I am God.'

'I am in the Father and the Father in me.'

'I [am] in my Father, and ye in me, and I in you.'

'The kingdom of God is within you.'

But nowhere in any of these great teachings, which are accepted by many as being authorities on God and on finding God, have I seen it state 'You cannot be Enlightened, or at one with God, or awaken etc, since there is nothing and nobody here to be or do anything!'. Can you see this?

153

Also, looking specifically at those who claim to be Enlightened and yet teach that there are lots of Enlightened (or un-Enlightened) beings floating about, I must say, 'Don't be so stupid...There is only one!! Have you not got that yet?' If you have indeed seen you are a part of one being, great. But it is premature to claim you are Enlightened until you have realised you ARE the one being and are living it each and every moment. Until then, you are still just one of many and are NOT Enlightened, which is why you are teaching that there are many!

With regards to the 'there's nobody here' teachings, I did wonder for a while where these came from and how our approaches could be so different. I then remembered one of my early insights as described on the page 'The Disappearing "I"', where I saw this is indeed like a dream or the eastern 'Maya', or illusion; that 'I' only exist 'here' because of the objects or forms 'appearing over there', and in truth neither have any substance. However, that was several years before I became 'this'. The insight that there is 'nothing here' is not Enlightenment. It's just one of the many insights that one may have on the way. You are not 'there' yet; and you know it, which is why you are saying there is no one here. When you do become the living truth, you will very definitely know you are here, even if you don't know what you are or where 'here' is; you will know you are it.

To be Enlightened, which is also known as 'Self-realisation' or 'God Realisation', does by definition require there to be a 'self' or a 'God' of some sort to realise and to be Enlightened. Until the above is realised, it is just an insight into the fact that this is an illusory temporary existence. When you truly become 'this' and all you experience is within you each and every moment, 'you' do not disappear as 'you' are all that is. You will only totally cease to be once there is no need for anything to exist and everything ends; even you. Until that time, this is all your creation, your being. Don't try and wash your hands of responsibility for it by saying you are not here, because you bloody well are! This is all you!

154

I always thought the truth was fixed. That a person who realised 'the truth' would know without any doubt what is true and how this all works. I heard my own teacher tell stories about existence and the end of the world etc and accepted that one day I would know that stuff too. I was asked today by someone (after telling him that I did not agree with the Buddhist teaching he had sent to me, which said that a person can come back as an animal), 'Nick, how do we know the dream will ever end?'

Best Guess Truth

The reason I did not agree that we can come back as an animal is that I do not accept anyone can go backwards, in the sense of Self-knowledge or Realisation; and I do not see that taking the body of a 'lesser' animal, which lacks the ability to reflect on its own awareness etc, would serve any purpose. That's what this page is about: How can different Enlightened teachers, all apparently in the experience of being 'at one' with life or 'God', contradict each other when describing this existence and explaining how it all works? Do they know or don't they? Who's telling the truth and who isn't? Are they lying or just delusional? As I experience it and see it here, it's like this…

A person realises that their own being is creating and sustaining all that is here, that this existence is their own dream and they are alone in this, but that's where the knowledge ends. From there on in it is down to logic and what I am calling here 'best guess truth' and even assumptions. This is a bit of a surprise to me, since it leaves space for different views of 'the truth', even between apparently Enlightened people. For instance, you have seen in previous pages that my own teacher taught 'It is every man and woman's RIGHT to be in this state!' and that this existence is moving towards a time where all will be living at this level of conscious awareness. He also described the emotion as being a parasite on the pure intellect and

155

we have other teachings that also see all this as false and a blight on the purity of being, saying it should all end as soon as possible. Many of these types tend to withdraw from society and often even from anything pleasurable, through fear of increasing their own attachment to this abomination (to them) of a sensory existence. We commonly see this in stories of monks and other holy people abstaining from 'the sins of the flesh'.

My own take on this is a bit different from the above. As you will have seen by now, I see nothing wrong with this existence, whether the individual is Enlightened or not, as it's all part of the dream and the dream provides what is needed to be experienced (whether seen as good or as bad); and as such I love the dream. I have no problem with the dream continuing, or with the dream ending. Either way, I accept what is and remain conscious, enjoying the experiences provided where I can. I am provided with a great life, by grace, and I neither tell you to wake up nor stay asleep. This is your life. I make no judgements about how it should be or about how you or I should be. Even once you are 'awake' in this existence, you are only aware you are dreaming. How you interpret that knowledge is still subjective. Love it, hate it or be indifferent to it, it continues nonetheless. As to how it all fits together and what is going to happen next? Well, to me, that's the 'best guess truth'. In the end it comes down to simply 'I am this', or even just 'I am', and you teach from there, however you see it.

I would like to add here too, that anything realised here is also only realised within this existence. If one accepts the first big realisation, that 'I' am dreaming this, this would also then seem to draw into question anything realised about what may be 'beyond' this, since one has already admitted one is dreaming. That is to say, even the realisation is dreamt, so the knowledge does seem to end with simply 'I am this', even with the knowledge that I don't know what 'this' is.

156

World Religions

The world consists of many societies and numerous religions, philosophies and teachings. There are also many divisions of the original teachings which have branched off to teach a slightly different focus or interpretation, with their own traditions, morals and beliefs.

I have touched on these in earlier pages and here I would like to print some more excerpts of a few of these religious teachings, as I have come across them. There have always been wars going on across the globe as to which is right and which is wrong, as if to kill another proves us right. However, you may see from reading some of the following pages that there is a common thread through most of them. I have tried to keep the works as unadulterated as possible. The extent to which this has been achieved may be debateable but I trust the point is not missed.

I do not have extensive knowledge of the various Buddhist teachings or traditions. I just know about Enlightenment and I understand the word Buddha means 'Enlightened One'. Here I wanted to have a look at the story of the Buddha and a few of his great teachings.

Buddhism

I was recently given a calendar of Zen sayings and have copied and posted a few entries below. These may be abbreviated versions of the originals so I apologise to any dedicated Buddhists for any offence caused. I have enjoyed reading these and they have shown me that what I teach is really nothing new, regardless of how original or even 'out there' it may seem to some. In fact my own story seems to be a similar path to that taken by the original Buddha, of searching for an end to suffering, eventually feeling the stillness within and becoming that. Here is his story as it has been reported...

The Buddha was born in approximately 566 BC with the name Siddhartha Gautama, a prince of the Sakya tribe of Nepal. The story says his father, the king, had been told by a wise man that his son would grow up to be either a great king or a great spiritual leader. The king, not wanting his son to be a spiritual leader, attempted to protect him from the outside world, keeping him within the palace grounds where possible and restricting his contact with the outside world, only permitting him to travel certain paths. It is said that, one day while returning home, the prince took a route other than the one set out for him and witnessed poverty and suffering which he had never seen before. He was horrified and vowed to find an end to this.

At twenty-nine years old, the prince left the comforts of his home, his wife and his family to seek the meaning of the suffering he saw around him. He explored and experimented with different teachings, all promising to show him the truth he sought. Several years of arduous yogic training followed, which involved abstinence from life's necessities as well as the luxuries he had enjoyed

161

throughout his youth. Finally Gautama abandoned the way of self-mortification and instead sat in (what became known as) 'mindful meditation' beneath a Bodhi tree, simply feeling the stillness within where there was 'nothing arising'. On the full moon of May, with the rising of the morning star, Siddhartha Gautama became the Buddha, the Enlightened One.

The Buddha wandered the plains of north-eastern India for a further forty-five years, teaching the path or Dharma he had realised in that moment. Around him developed a community or Sangha of monks, and later nuns, drawn from every tribe and caste, devoted to practising this path. It is said, in approximately 486 BC at the age of eighty, the Buddha died. His last words are recorded as being: 'Impermanent are all created things. Strive on with awareness.' Below are a few sayings which have been attributed to the Buddha:

'Within this fathom-long body is found all the teachings, is found suffering, the cause of suffering, and the end of suffering.'

'Only within our own body, with its heart and mind, can bondage and suffering be found, and only here can we find true liberation.'

'Those who are un-awakened grasp their thoughts and feelings, their body, their perceptions and consciousness, and take them as solid, separate from the rest. Those who are awakened have the same thoughts and feelings, perceptions, body and consciousness, but they are not grasped, not held, not taken as oneself.'

'It is our very search for perfection outside ourselves that causes our suffering.'

'One moment, ten thousand years, one moment.'

'We are what we think. All that we are arises with our thoughts. With our thoughts, we make our world.'

'Like the arrow-smith who turns his arrows straight and true, a wise person makes his character straight and true.'

'If you use your mind to look for a Buddha, you won't see the Buddha. As long as you look for a Buddha somewhere else, you'll

162

never see that your own mind is the Buddha. Don't use a Buddha to worship a Buddha and don't use your mind to invoke the Buddha.

'Buddhas don't recite sutras. Buddhas don't keep precepts, and Buddhas don't break precepts. Buddhas don't keep or break anything. Buddhas don't do good or evil. To find a Buddha, you have to see your own nature. Whoever sees his own nature is a Buddha...'

'The Buddha was wandering through India shortly after his Enlightenment. Several men encountered him and sensed something quite extraordinary about the handsome monk.
    "Are you a God?" they asked.
    "No," he answered.
    "Well, are you a Deva or an angel?"
    "No."
    "Some kind of wizard or magician?"
    "No," he said again.
    Finally, perplexed, the men asked, "Well, what are you?"
    "I am awake," he answered.'

'Awakening is not something newly discovered; it has always existed. There is no need to seek or follow the advice of others. Learn to listen to that voice within yourself just here and now. Your body and mind will become clear and you will realise the unity of all things. Do not doubt the possibilities because of the simplicity of these teachings. If you can't find the truth right where you are, where else do you think you will find it?'

'A guru is like a fire. If you get too close you get burned; if you stay too far away, you don't get enough heat.'

'People with opinions just go around bothering one another.'

'You are the light, you are the refuge, there is no place to take shelter but yourself.' (Inscription over the Buddha's ashes).

I have been told, of all the branches of Buddhism, Zen is the nearest to the original teaching. I did not know this but found a few Zen sayings I did like...

Zen sayings

"The religion before religion." (One definition of Zen)

"When the pupil is ready to learn, a teacher will appear."

"To understand God is to listen to Jesus and Mohammed and Buddha; but don't get caught up in names. Listen beyond them; listen to God's breath."

"The wonderful thing about Zen practice is that you do it whether you like it or not."

"The only practice that is worthwhile is to ask: 'What is this?' WHAT IS THIS?"

"Gaining Enlightenment is an accident. Spiritual practice simply makes us accident prone."

"To follow the path, look to the Master, follow the Master, walk with the Master, see through the Master, become the Master."

"No snowflake falls in an inappropriate place."

"Above the saddle, no rider. Below the saddle, no horse."

"The trouble is that you think you have time."

"A clearly Enlightened person falls into the well. How is this so?"

"After the ecstasy, the laundry."

"A samurai once asked Zen Master Hakuin where he would go after he died. Hakuin answered 'How am I supposed to know?'
'How do you know? You're a Zen master!' exclaimed the samurai.
'Yes, but not a dead one,' Hakuin answered."

"Do not seek the truth, only cease to cherish your opinions."

"It takes a wise man to learn from his mistakes, but an even wiser man to learn from others."

164

"The ten thousand questions are one question. If you cut through the one question, then the ten thousand questions disappear."

"The tighter you squeeze the less you have."

"The ways to the one are as many as the lives of men."

"To do a certain kind of thing, you have to be a certain kind of person."

"To know that there is nothing to know, and to grieve that it is so difficult to communicate this 'nothing to know' to others – this is the life of Zen, this is the deepest thing in the world."

"When you reach the top, keep climbing."

A few Zen stories

"A monk asked his master: 'How are you when death arrives?'
The master replied: 'When served tea, I take tea. When served a meal, I take a meal.'"

"A beginning student complained to his master that his meditation practice of following the breath was boring. The Zen master unexpectedly grabbed the student and held his head under the water for quite a long time while the student struggled to come up. Finally he let the student go. 'Now how boring is your breath?' he asked."

"An eager Zen student arrived at the temple. He sought out the Master and said: 'I want to join your community and attain Enlightenment. How long will it take me?'
    'Ten years,' the Master replied.
    'How about if I really work hard, and double my efforts?'
    'Then twenty years,' the Master said.
    'That's not fair! Why did you double it?'
    After which the Master said: 'In your case, I'm afraid it will be thirty years.'"

"Once when Yakusan was sitting, Sekito saw him and asked: 'What are you doing here?'
    Yakusan said: 'I'm not doing anything.'
    Sekito said: 'Then you are just sitting idly.'

'If I were sitting idly, that would be doing something,' Yakusan said.

'You said you are not doing,' Sekito said. 'What is it that you are not doing?'

'Even the saints don't know,' said Yakusan."

"A monk asked Yun-men: 'What does "sitting correctly contemplating true reality" really mean?'

Yun-men answered: 'A coin lost in the river is found in the river.'"

"A student was walking through a pine forest with a Zen Master. 'Please,' the disciple begged, 'tell me about Enlightenment.'

'See that tree,' the Master said, pointing, 'See how tall it is?'

'Yes,' the student said.

Then the master pointed to a different tree. 'See how short this tree is?' he asked.

'Yes,' said the student.

'That is Enlightenment,' the Master replied."

"Once Fa-yen was asked, 'What is the first principle?'
He answered: 'If I should tell you, it would become the second principle.'"

"Before a person studies Zen, mountains are mountains and waters are waters. After the first glimpse into the truth of Zen, mountains are no longer mountains and waters are not waters. After Enlightenment, mountains are once again mountains and waters once again waters."

"The platform sutra:
Sentient beings are immobile.
Inanimate objects are stationary.
He who trains himself by exercise to be motionless gets no benefit other than making him as still as an inanimate object."

"The Third Patriarch
True Enlightenment and wholeness arise when we are without anxiety about non-perfection."

166

Sayings from various sources...

'What do you want to get Enlightened for? You may not like it.' (Shunryu Suzuki)

'It is the intensity of the longing that does all the work.' (Kabir)

'The important point of spiritual practice is not to try to escape your life, but to face it exactly and completely.' (Dainin Katagiri)

'Birds chirp, dogs run, mountains are high, valleys low. It's all perfect wisdom! The seasons change, the stars shine in the heavens; it's perfect wisdom. Regardless of whether we realise it or not, we are always in the midst of the Way; or more strictly speaking, we are nothing but the Way itself.' (Taizan Maezumi)

'The fundamental delusion of reality is to suppose that I am here and you are out there.' (Yasutani)

'The moment between before and after is called Truth.' (Katagiri Roshi)

'In Zazen, the self does the self by the self.' (Master Sawaki)

'There's no point in translating all of the old Chinese texts – not if you're serious about understanding real Zen. The sound of the rain needs no translation.' (Morimoto Roshi)

'Most people think that we live in the actual world while we are alive, and that after we take the last breath we somehow wander into a vague realm of the spirit. It is a great mistake to see two separate realms. Instead, where we live is in fact the spiritual realm, a realm of many billion worlds, which goes beyond three, four, or even infinite dimensions. Then the danger is that we might think that this is a realm that is empty and boundless. Watch out! It's all manifested right here at this moment. It is alive and kicking!' (Soen Nakagawa)

'Do not recite sutras. Do not make portraits of me. Just bury my body in the back mountains. It is enough that you cover me with earth.' (Takuan, final wishes to his students)

'Whatever you think is delusion.' (Katagiri Roshi)

'Only our own searching for happiness prevents us from seeing it. It is like a vivid rainbow which you pursue without ever catching it, or a dog chasing its own tail. Although peace and happiness do not exist as an actual thing or place, they are always available and accompanying you every instant.' (Gendun Rinpoche)

'It's amazing, a wonder, that one wakes up in the morning.' (Nagarjuna)

'To find perfect composure in the midst of change is to find nirvana.' (Shunryu Suzuki)

'Having no destination, I am never lost.' (Ikkyu)

'It is important to see that the main point of any spiritual practice is to step out of the bureaucracy of ego. This means stepping out of ego's constant desire for a higher, more spiritual, more transcendental version of knowledge, religion, virtue, judgement, comfort or whatever it is that the particular ego is seeking.' (Chogyam Trungpa)

'When you find your place, practice begins.' (Dogen)

'Not knowing how near the truth is, we seek it far away.' (Harkuin)

'In the entire ten directions of the Buddha's universe, there is only one way. When we see clearly, there is no difference in the teachings. What is there to lose? What is there to gain? If we gain something, it was there from the beginning. If we lose something, it was hidden nearby.' (Ryokan)

'The greatest sin is to be unconscious.' (Carl Gustav Jung)

'A Zendo is not a place for bliss and relaxation. It is a furnace room for the combustion of our delusion. What tools do we need to use? Only one. We've all heard it, yet we use it very seldom. It is called "attention."' (Charlotte Joko Beck)

'Zen does not confuse spirituality with thinking about God while one is peeling potatoes. Zen spirituality is just to peel the potatoes.' (Alan Watts)

'Those who are awake live in a state of constant amazement.' (Jack Kornfield)

168

'At the very least, sitting Zen practice, called zazen, will bring about a strong sense of well-being as the clutter of ideas and emotions falls away and body and mind return to natural harmony with all creation. Out of this emptiness can come a true insight into the nature of existence, which is no different from one's own nature. To travel this path one need not be a "Zen Buddhist", which is only another idea to be discarded, like "Enlightenment" and like "the Buddha" and like "God".' (Peter Matthiessen)

'To be nobody but yourself in a world which is doing its best to make you everybody else means to fight the hardest human battle ever and never to stop fighting.' (E.E. Cummings)

'Bring yourself back to the point quite gently. Even if you do nothing during the whole of your hour but bring your heart back a thousand times, though it went away every time you brought it back, your hour would be very well employed.' (St Francis De Sales, on meditation)

'Each second is a universe of time.' (Henry Miller)

'Wherever you are, you are in Zendo.' (Bernie Glassman)

A few Buddhist stories...

"There were two monks who had been on a pilgrimage away from the monastery and were on their way home. They approached a small river which had to be crossed and on the bank was a woman looking for some way to cross the water without getting wet. The monks were forbidden from having any physical contact with women, so the first monk walked past the woman and proceeded to wade across.

The second hesitated, then offered the woman a lift on his back across the river. She accepted and the monk carried her across. Once on the other side both monks continued their journey in silence. A day and a half passed and neither of the monks spoke. Finally the other could hold out no longer. 'I don't believe you did that. You touched that woman. I am going to have to report you when we get back!'

'Are you still carrying her?' The first replied. 'I put her down at the river!'"

"The young monk was on his way to the bedside of his dying Master. He had worked hard for years to live as well as possible the 'Enlightened Way' and hoped his Master would announce him the new Master to take over the teaching of others after his death.

The monk entered the Master's house, removed his shoes as was the normal practice and made his way through the house to his Master's bedside.

The old Master looked at him as he approached, and asked simply, 'Which side of the door did you leave your shoes?'

The young monk could not remember and knew he was not ready to take on the position, as he had not been conscious when he had removed his shoes."

"There was a great Master holding a talk on an island and many people were attending. During the talk in which questions were invited from the eager attendees, a man stood up and announced he was so spiritually advanced that he had walked across the water to get there. 'Why?' asked the Master. 'You could have got the boat for three rupees.'"

The Bhagavad-Gita, for those not familiar with it, is the 'holy' book of the Hindus and the Hare-Krishnas (apologies if there are others).

I first read the Bhagavad-Gita soon after beginning my spiritual search. There are over eight hundred pages with the purports or explanations beneath each translation and I read a hundred pages per day after college, completing the book in little over a week. Recently I read the translations again.

Bhagavad-Gita

The story describes Arjuna, a great warrior and leader, in his chariot overlooking the battlefield where two armies were ready to fight. With friends on both sides, Arjuna began to doubt his ability to lead his people into battle. As he voiced his concerns to his charioteer, Krishna, it was revealed to Arjuna that he, Krishna, Arjuna's long-term friend and family member, was actually the embodiment of the supreme personality or Godhead.

The Bhagavad-Gita is the discourse between Arjuna and Krishna, as Krishna teaches Arjuna that there is no death for the soul; that the cycle of birth and death continues until there is no need. He goes on to explain how a person is able to realise this whilst in a body, teaching the simplest way is 'devotional service to Me'. The text further explains devotional service is any action, whatever it be, even if it is killing if that is what you do, whilst in the remembrance of the supreme personality, 'Me'. Lastly, and most importantly, Krishna pointed out that the supreme personality, which he refers to as 'Me', is the consciousness within each living thing.

Some say the entire story is metaphorical or mythological, describing the inner turmoil that goes on with the individual. The following are direct quotes from the translated *Bhagavad-Gita – As It Is*. You may notice the obvious similarities between some of the Buddhist teachings above as well as my own. The numbers relate to their position in the book translated by His Divine grace A.C. Bhaktivedanta Swami Prabhupada.

3.3 'The Supreme Personality of Godhead said: O sinless Arjuna, I have already explained that there are two classes of men who try to realise the self. Some are inclined to understand it by empirical, philosophical speculation and others by devotional service.'

3.4 'Not by merely abstaining from work can one achieve freedom from reaction, nor by renunciation alone can one attain perfection.'

3.17 'But for one who takes pleasure in the self, whose human life is one of self-realisation, and who is satisfied in the self only, fully satiated—for him there is no duty.'

3.18 'A self-realised man has no purpose to fulfil in the discharge of his prescribed duties, nor has he any reason not to perform such work. Nor has he any need to depend on any other living being.'

3.19 'Therefore, without being attached to the fruits of activities, one should act as a matter of duty, for by working without attachment one attains the Supreme.'

5.3 'One who neither hates nor desires the fruits of his activities is known to be always renounced. Such a person, free from all dualities, easily overcomes material bondage and is completely liberated, O mighty-armed Arjuna.'

5.6 'Merely renouncing all activities yet not engaging in the devotional service of the Lord cannot make one happy. But a thoughtful person engaged in devotional service can achieve the Supreme without delay.'

5.8/9 'A person in the divine consciousness, although engaged in seeing, hearing, touching, smelling, eating, moving about, sleeping and breathing, always knows within himself that he actually does nothing at all. Because while speaking, evacuating, receiving, or opening or closing his eyes, he always knows that only the material senses are engaged with their objects and that he is aloof from them.'

5.17 'When one's intelligence, mind, faith and refuge are all fixed in the Supreme, then one becomes fully cleansed of misgivings through complete knowledge and thus proceeds straight on the path of liberation.'

5.19 'Those whose minds are established in sameness and equanimity have already conquered the conditions of birth and death. They are flawless like Brahman, and thus they are already situated in Brahman.'

5.24 'One whose happiness is within, who is active and rejoices within, and whose aim is inward is actually the perfect mystic. He is liberated in the Supreme, and ultimately he attains the Supreme.'

6.6 'For him who has conquered the mind, the mind is the best of friends; but for one who has failed to do so, his mind will remain the greatest enemy.'

6.26 'From wherever the mind wanders due to its flickering and unsteady nature, one must certainly withdraw it and bring it back under the control of the self.'

6.27 'The yogi whose mind is fixed on Me verily attains the highest perfection of transcendental happiness. He is beyond the mode of passion, he realises his qualitative identity with the Supreme, and thus he is freed from all reactions to past deeds.'

6.29 'A true yogi observes Me in all beings and also sees every being in Me. Indeed, the self-realised person sees Me, the same Supreme Lord, everywhere.'

6.30 'For one who sees Me everywhere and sees everything in Me, I am never lost, nor is he ever lost to Me.'

9.30 'Even if one commits the most abominable action, if he is engaged in devotional service he is to be considered saintly because he is properly situated in his determination.'

9.32 'O son of Pritha, those who take shelter in Me, though they be of lower birth – women, vaishyas [merchants] and shudras [workers] – can attain the supreme destination.'

9.34 'Engage your mind always in thinking of Me, become My devotee, offer obeisances to Me and worship Me. Being completely absorbed in Me, surely you will come to Me.'

10.20 'I am the Supersoul, O Arjuna, seated in the hearts of all living entities. I am the beginning, the middle and the end of all beings.'

12.8 'Just fix your mind upon Me, the Supreme Personality of Godhead, and engage all your intelligence in Me. Thus you will live in Me always, without a doubt.'

13.15 'The Supersoul is the original source of all senses, yet He is without senses. He is unattached, although He is the maintainer of all living beings. He transcends the modes of nature, and at the same time He is the master of all the modes of material nature.'

13.16 'The Supreme Truth exists outside and inside of all living beings, the moving and the non-moving. Because He is subtle, He is beyond the power of the material senses to see or to know. Although far, far away, He is also near to all.'

13.17 'Although the Supersoul appears to be divided among all beings, He is never divided. He is situated as one. Although He is the maintainer of every living entity, it is to be understood that He devours and develops all.'

13.18 'He is the source of light in all luminous objects. He is beyond the darkness of matter and is un-manifested. He is knowledge, He is the object of knowledge, and He is the goal of knowledge. He is situated in everyone's heart.'

13.35 'Those who see with eyes of knowledge the difference between the body and the knower of the body, and can also understand the process of liberation from bondage in material nature, attain to the supreme goal.'

14.2 'By becoming fixed in this knowledge, one can attain to the transcendental nature like My own. Thus established, one is not born at the time of creation or disturbed at the time of dissolution.'

15.15 'I am seated in everyone's heart, and from Me come remembrance, knowledge and forgetfulness. By all the Vedas, I am to be known. Indeed, I am the compiler of Vedanta, and I am the knower of the Vedas.'

18.61 'The Supreme Lord is situated in everyone's heart, O Arjuna, and is directing the wanderings of all living entities, who are seated as on a machine, made of the material energy.'

Many of us in the West are familiar with much of the Bible. We are taught at school of Jesus' teachings of forgiveness, 'love thy neighbour as thyself' and 'let he who is without sin cast the first stone', to name a couple. We don't adhere to much of it and those of us who try to often do so with judgement, both of ourselves and others, so really fall short before we start.

The Bible

Some believe the Bible to be historical fact. Others, perhaps cynically, see the stories as being no more than a means to control the masses. Some scholars even seem to have proof that the Bible and the stories of Jesus are usurped pagan stories; such as described in the book *The Jesus Mysteries* written by Timothy Freke. It has also been said that much of the truth within the Bible has long since been removed to protect the Church's interests, since the teachings were of finding the truth within your own body with no need to go through a priest.

Whatever the truth is, some elements of the teachings do remain relevant to the inner spiritual search we are looking at here, as opposed to praying to some far-off God to get to a future paradise after death. This is less surprising when we consider, if the Bible stories do have a pagan origin, that it is said there was a portion of pagan myth which went into the subject of Self-realisation and oneness with all existence within one's own body; which is exactly what we are looking at here.

In the Bhagavad-Gita we have seen Krishna use the term 'Me' throughout, when talking about the Supreme Personality or Godhead, and qualifying this further by saying this is within each and every living thing and containing instructions as to how a person can come to know this. So, following this line, and considering that many do accept the Christian God as omnipotent and therefore indeed in everything, perhaps the term 'I' or 'me' when apparently spoken by

Jesus in his teachings has the same meaning: that is, the essence within each person and not just himself.

In the same way as the story of the battle in the Bhagavad-Gita has been said to be representative of the internal struggle, looking at the Bible, the story describes the 'Son of God', the son of the creator of all existence, even God himself in form, as he tries to teach the world about oneness and love. Eventually he surrenders, allowing those he tried to heal to crucify him, the nails literally pinning him to existence, at which point he leaves his body to become spirit, returning to the source again to be 'at one' with the father. This could also be a powerful representation of the inner struggle of the spiritual life: No matter how hard one fights, in the end one can only surrender to what is, at which point one is freed.

Below are a few more quotes from the Bible

John 10:30 'I and the Father are one.'

John 14:6 'Jesus said to him, 'I am the way, and the truth, and the life; no one comes to the Father, but through Me.'

Psalms 46:10 'Be still, and know that I am God.'

John 14:10 'Believest thou not that I am in the Father, and the Father in me? The words that I speak unto you I speak not of myself: but the Father that dwelleth in me, he doeth the works.'

John 14:20 'At that day ye shall know that I [am] in my Father, and ye in me, and I in you.'

John 8:58 'Jesus said unto them, Verily, verily, I say unto you, Before Abraham was, I am.'

Matthew 28:18–20 'And lo I am with you always, even unto the end of the world. Amen.'

Luke 17:21 'The kingdom of God is within you.'

☯ ॐ ✡ ☸ ☾ ✝

I could hardly not mention the Koran, the holy book of the Islamic and Muslim faith, when looking at a few of the world's major religions and in light of the current climate. Few Westerners have read the Koran, perhaps most have never even seen a copy, yet the subject has been of major controversy in recent times as there are public disputes as to what is actually said in the holy book.

The Koran

When comparing the other religions or teachings with that contained within the Koran, there is one major difference which is apparent: The others follow, or describe, the teachings of a man who claimed to be 'at one' with God, or the 'Godhead' itself, or at least to have found the end of suffering and the end of time and existence within his own body whilst alive.

The Koran tells of the Prophet Mohammed, a wise spiritual man and leader who spent much time meditating and praying alone in a cave. The story says, either whilst sleeping or in a trance, Mohammed received the instruction from the angel Gabriel, who was speaking directly from Allah, God: 'Recite!' The order was repeated three times. The Koran is said to be a compilation of the directions that Gabriel proceeded to give to Mohammed.

The Koran teaches of the oneness of God, but unlike the others it is not a book describing how to find peace within oneself and Self-Realisation or union with God whilst alive. Instead it describes the war-torn times in which it was written where Mohammed and his followers were persecuted, and gives instructions on how to live correctly. It is clear times were tough, certainly when reading particular excerpts, and it is understandable how there is the current confusion between what are called 'fundamentalists' and the 'modern-day' Muslims who enjoy the relative peace and the general diversity of many of our cultures today.

I am not going to go into details here, but I do invite you to get hold of a copy and read it, if you are interested, so you do not need to debate and dispute from hearsay and misinformation. Most of us are unable to read the original text so we do have to rely on English translations, of which there may be many. As well as my own copy mentioned below, I have been fortunate to have seen one owned by a good friend from Turkey and another copy belonging to a friend from Africa, both devout Muslims, neither of whom could read the original text and had to rely on their translations and, like many of us with the Bible, have only been taught certain excerpts and obtained 'a taste' of the message from these. It is the deeper messages which describe life in the warring times which the so-called 'fundamentalists' follow, much of which it seems some modern-day Muslims have never seen or heard before (according to the friends I have spoken with). And therefore it is sometimes disputed whether the teachings exist at all, as it does not fit into the modern understanding of the word of God they follow. The synopsis below is the synopsis from my own copy, translated by N.J. Dawood and published by Penguin Classics.

Koran

The Koran, as N.J. Dawood states, is 'not only one of the most influential books of prophetic literature but also a literary masterpiece in its own right'.

Universally accepted by Muslims to be the infallible word of God as revealed to Mohammed by the angel Gabriel nearly fourteen hundred years ago, the Koran still provides the rules of conduct fundamental to the Arab way of life. N.J. Dawood's masterly translation, first published in the mid-1950s and now completely revised in the light of a life-long study of the language and style of the Koran, presents the English reader with a clear, fluent and authoritative rendering, while fully reflecting the characteristic flavour and rhythm of the original. The present edition follows the original sequence of the Koranic suras, and is provided with a comprehensive index.

You may have noticed the similarities in the religions Buddhism, Hinduism and Christianity, where we are directed to go within our own body to find the ultimate truth. It is described as stillness or the Supersoul, or the Godhead, or 'Me', or 'I', or God, or Brahman, or in the immortal words 'Whoever sees his own nature is a Buddha'.

Summary

I teach 'Be aware of where you are and of what you are feeling', but as you can see, it's really nothing new. It is just another way of directing you to be aware of what is, to not get seduced into the mind with its imaginings and feelings, or to not want anything beyond what you are experiencing at any given moment. I quoted the sections of the above religions because there is so much debate and confusion, even between branches of the same religion, and I would like to show there really is no need. First, if all is indeed 'one', then who are we arguing with? Second, since they all say the truth is the space in you and it is your own true nature which is the thing you are seeking, what is there to argue about?

Whatever you do, wherever you live and however hard you try to achieve, to learn and to grow, I have written this book with the aim of demonstrating you are alright. You are exactly where you are supposed to be, doing exactly what you are supposed to do. How do I know this?…Because you are doing it. That's proof enough for me. There is only 'one' here, and you are it. Who else could it be? If it is time to change, in any way, then change, and that would be right too. This is your life, your game, and you are the player and the board on which it is played. You cannot lose. You can only keep going.

The Journey
Continues...

This book has been a bit of a journey, demonstrating my first three years in this new place, which perhaps isn't really a place at all and certainly isn't new. As you will have seen, it is the original state beyond and behind all that is, and as such is beyond this thing we call time or existence. There is no sequence of events here, in the stillness within; at least none that we have access to. There is simply being what I am (what you are), and living that.

To finish off on a light note, this last section is a bit of fun for me. The first topic is a speculative look at the future of the human race and perhaps a look back at those who may have gone before. The second, 'Breaking the Magician's Code', compares my teaching with a TV show of the same name and suggests why it can be necessary to hear the truth time and time again, until it becomes one's own truth. I hope you have enjoyed this book. Thank you

☯ ॐ ✡ ☸ ☪ ✝

Okay, now the fun bit: This piece has nothing to do with finding one's self, or the truth, or becoming at one with God. It is just one person's look at the world and how things work, and linking these to a few scientific findings and reports and coming out with a hypothesis. Being 'awake' or 'Enlightened', or whatever else you may wish to call it, does not give one all the answers to the universe, as we have seen. It simply awards a stronger sense of 'self' and a knowledge that this all exists within the one experiencing it; but it must still be lived or explored.

The Future of Mankind

Some years ago I developed an interest in UFOs, alien spacecraft, sightings, crashes, alien bodies and the like. For a while I subscribed to a couple of magazines focusing on this area and bought a book which explored in detail many of the various reports, including documents which had been released by the government thanks to the disclosure laws. However, it was not long before one sighting became similar to the other forty or so I had read previously and I lost interest.

This interest was rekindled a little when watching a documentary recently about the ruins of an ancient city discovered hidden within the Amazon. The walls were huge and the city boundary enormous and yet, from the condition of the remains and plant growth, it was clear the structure goes back many thousands of years. The scientists, on studying the area, said they were pretty sure the destruction had happened due to the people of the time destroying too much of the rainforest with the expansion of their civilisation, causing flooding (sound familiar?). So, who were these people and how is it that they were building such cities so long ago? Well, I have a far out, outrageous theory: No, not aliens exactly.

In my days of reading about aliens, there were also stories of the remains of structures that had been found on the moon. (Again, if

183

you have not heard these before and this is not your cup of tea, then this is all likely to be a bit difficult to read, but as I said, it's just a bit of fun.) As I watched this programme about the ruins in the Amazon, I began to put all these bits of information together and something occurred to me:

It is said we are heading towards self-annihilation, with the human race overpopulating the earth, destroying the rainforests and the ozone layer and polluting the seas etc. What is to happen to us? And what happened to those who were before? Can you see where this is going? Are we going round in full circle?

By full circle I mean this: We have seen and are seeing the evolution of the animal kingdom, as it develops or evolves into a creature such that can create great machinery, lords over the entire planet and makes major scientific advancements (us); until finally destroying much of the planet, and perhaps themselves. However, the idea I put forward in this section is that this will not happen before they have advanced enough to make spaceships able to leave the planet they are destroying, and off they go (some of them anyway); a little like Noah's ark in the Bible story.

When the earth is unable to sustain human life any longer and all have gone, relieved at having got rid of the offspring that almost wiped out all life, the earth spends the next several thousand years recovering, removing almost all trace of what went before and restoring the natural balance. In the meantime the original occupants who have left are off exploring the galaxy (or trying to survive in space, depending on one's perspective).

As the earth recovers, it is again generating a species similar to that which almost destroyed it, since that is the way of life: evolution and survival of the fittest. Soon this new species is exploring the environment, again multiplying to a point which is not sustainable, stripping the planet bare of resources and polluting it to a point which will take millennia to repair. These new beings believe arrogantly, not only thinking that they are the only ones in the galaxy but also that they are the original intelligent occupants of this planet which existed millions and millions of years before they did. They are bewildered when they do find what seem to be remains of civilisations which

184

existed long before their own records dictate, and these are put down as 'just another mystery'. They also begin to share stories of other beings in vast spaceships visiting their planet, but most dismiss these too as just foolish science-fiction. They head towards their own destruction, but as it's going to be long after those alive today have gone, besides some token gestures from a few they are not really worried.

As progress happens and their own space programme develops, the first thing they do is make a base on the moon which is the nearest planet to them. Here, since the gravity is so much less, is a perfect place from which to launch further explorations as they do not have to fight with the earth's atmosphere at every take-off. Soon the earth is all but uninhabitable (as it was before them) and the new space creatures continue their development outwards into the galaxy.

Time passes. The earth again begins to recover. It's not long before the space-beings have lost any pigment due to very little exposure to sunlight. Their eyes have begun to expand to catch all traces of light and their bodies have become thin from the lack of gravity in space. (Does this sound like the aliens known as the 'Greys', which are described in many of the stories and sightings?)

They return home at times to the planet they all but destroyed lifetimes ago, and monitor the development of the new life. Existence continues in cycles, always evolving, or revolving, and never-ending, with each evolutionary generation on earth believing they are the first, or the last, and each following the one before. This really is 'life without end'.

So, to summarise, my suggestion is: Could these so-called aliens, if they do exist, be the ancestors of previous inhabitants of earth, and thus themselves be previous earthlings?

Don't worry too much about this. If the idea behind this has ever been said before, I have never heard or read it. This is only one person's theory, putting together fragments of scientific findings, theories and ideas, with a background of Self-realisation to give a solid foundation of logic and clarity. Existence tends to reflect or symbolise the reality 'within' and the theory above does serve to

185

represent the nature of attachment which has brought this world to flourish. The inhabitants of the earth strive outwards, away from their centre and their source, and further into creation. The individual drives outwards away from the self, with the need for more emotional stimulation, and the universe is itself said to be expanding outwards. Maybe another example of things expanding is in the ultimate evolution of the earth, in the form of a being which leaves its home planet to go on developing elsewhere; everything expanding outwards, away from the centre.

There is nothing to be proven by this piece. There is no moral to this story and no lesson to help to realise who or what you are. Even if the above is true, throughout all of it, life is the same. It is the awareness: looking out and experiencing all that happens. Whether it is sitting in the park, living on a space-station on the moon or whizzing around the universe in flying saucers, it's all the same awareness. It is the one reading this now. Do you feel it? Because you are it! Do not allow the mind with its thoughts and emotions to keep expanding outwards away from the centre, away from yourself...not if you want to know the peace of being complete in the centre where all is still. That's where 'you' are. That's where it all begins.

Occasionally a thought will occur to me, of another way to describe something or to explain it to make it clearer. In a conversation today I found myself likening my teaching to the programme on television *Breaking the Magician's Code* and how it relates to what I teach:

Breaking the Magician's Code

You may have seen this program. It hosts a masked magician who performs amazing death-defying feats on stage, just as a world class magician would with an audience, and then proceeds to demonstrate very simply and clearly how it is done, showing all camera angles and close-ups. I have always been entertained by magic and felt I had to watch the first few episodes of this programme when it came on, but as I did so something changed.

While watching it, I almost felt cheated, not because I had been shown how the apparently amazing trick was performed, but at how simple (often painfully so) it was to perform, and with very little expertise at all. What had looked really amazingly clever was actually the result of no more than camera angles or clever props. But is this anything new? No, not really. However, if you are like me, you may like to be amazed, and like to wonder at how such impossible tricks are performed in front of an audience, who are all hopelessly looking for the catch. I had assumed as I sat and watched that the magician must be highly skilled, talented or clever, and that the illusions would require many years of preparation. At times this may be the case, but for a large percentage, as shown on the programme, anyone having watched it would now know how it is done, and could perhaps get up on stage and perform the trick every bit as efficiently as the magician.

Now we come to the other amazing part for me: Having watched how the trick is done, and almost felt disgust at the apparent deceit at making me think they were 'special', or at least clever, I may turn on the television some weeks or months later to watch the same trick

187

being performed by another magician, with all the glamour and zest, and I fall for it again. I may even turn to the person next to me and say, 'I watched a programme once about how they do this, but I cannot remember it now. I just know it was very simple!' But if it was so simple, how come I cannot remember how it was done? I had watched it carefully and it had had a strong effect on me at the time. What had happened?

So what happened and how does this relate to my own teaching? Well, I address in my books and teachings a subject which has eluded the vast majority of the world's greatest scientists, philosophers and spiritual teachers, and answer questions every human being on the planet is likely to ask at some point, perhaps in their darkest moments. Many are convinced that no one can ever really know the answers they seek. I explain the process and describe the path in such an amazingly simple way that it may seem to lose some of its magnificence and mystery, and is almost blatantly obvious when seen. And when it is seen, what then? The person is likely to sense there is something to this and yet it seems almost too terrifyingly simple. It threatens to undo all they have believed and accepted as real to date, and as such it cannot be held on to for long by the mind that wants to be mystified; it wants to be amazed and believe that it is witnessing what cannot be known or understood. What was briefly seen is forgotten just as quickly and they return to their path of searching, perhaps retaining some piece of memory of the time that someone once claimed to understand it and have the answers, but for some reason they cannot remember now what it was all about. The world is still full of mystery for them, and pain and loss, as they struggle on with the belief that no one can really know what this is all about. When it is time for them really to know, to live the role of the magician and see through the illusion, the knowledge will again be there. They will again be amazed at how it is done, as if seeing it for the first time, but this time it does not spoil the illusion for them as it did before, but instead they marvel at the simplicity and the effectiveness. Seeing through the illusion no longer spoils the enjoyment, instead awarding a new sense of appreciation for the wonder that is experienced, in knowledge, not ignorance.

188

There are many possible lessons in the above, whether it is to see that there is no need to judge those who still enjoy the illusion; whether it is not to judge oneself when for some reason you don't seem to get it straight away, or when you later forget what you thought you understood or had experienced...whatever it is, it doesn't matter. As in the words which came to me some years ago now 'A dream it may be, but the dream goes on', whether this is an illusion, a dream, or whether you realise it or not, it is still here and it still must be lived. All you have to do is live it. There is no escape and there is no failure here. You are always in the right place, doing what you need to be doing; so keep going. Life is always working with you. Eventually you will get to see the rules of the game behind this life, or put another way, you will see how the magician does his tricks. It was all for your entertainment anyway.

Acknowledgments

A big thank you to all who have contacted me over the last few years, asking questions and sharing their stories in the search for some truth behind them. It is through experiences that we grow and the learning continues, even once one appears to have finished.

Thank you also to those who helped prepare this book, with proofreading and various suggestions, and particularly to Paul Berryman who has done a wonderful job with the cover.

I am most grateful too for Timothy Freke and Jordan Gruber, who managed to spare time out of their hectic schedules in responding to my contact, looking over the manuscript and being willing to write a few words for the cover. Thank you both.

A book like this is never the result of one person's work. The information itself requires a lifetime of experiences, of interacting and learning, and then come the practicalities of creating the written work. I suspect there will be many more books, CDs and very likely DVDs in the coming future (accepting that time exists), through which I will be able to describe the ongoing experience. Please continue to visit the website and contact us for more information.

Thank you,

Nick Roach

Also by Nick Roach: *Enlightenment, the Simple Path*
                       NR Publishing, 2010

For information on Nick's talks, teaching classes, one-to-ones and other publications:

Please visit: www.nickroach.co.uk
Email: in@nickroach.co.uk

About the Author

Nick Roach was born on 12th June 1973. His childhood was not particularly different from many other children, having some sort of emotional difficulty (not diagnosed as being dyslexic until his late 30s), and between the ages nine and fifteen Nick was at boarding school. However, from his childhood Nick did possess a natural ability to see solutions to problems and an innate need to know and understand why things happen.

By the time Nick was fifteen years old he had begun to ask why life was so painful. He saw people around him unhappy and fighting and he too struggled with emotional difficulties, and yet everyone seemed to accept these without question. It was like living in a nightmare of a world where everyone is unhappy and no one thinks to question why.

Having looked into numerous paranormal and new-age practices in his search for answers for a couple of years, buying books on every subject he could find, finally Nick gave up. At seventeen he threw the metaphorical gauntlet down to life, demanding that he be shown that there was a reason for this as he was not prepared to play the game any longer, without knowing why. He arranged a sitting with a psychic in the last hope that this person would have the answers he needed. This was to be the turning point for Nick.

The psychic told him he was already on a high spiritual level and that this was the cause of his distress, and he

193

would develop very quickly if he wanted to, but he didn't have to. Nick knew he did. He had no choice.

After a year or so of practising meditation and analysing and questioning every thought or feeling that entered him, Nick found the teachings of a Western Master named Barry Long, who taught simply 'Stillness is the Way'.

Nick battled on, every day fighting to hold the stillness within as the emotion fought to take him off into the imaginary hell; week after week, month after month, year after year, with Nick repeatedly asking 'How long...how long?' until he no longer asked. Thirteen years had passed and finally all the insights and experiences came together in one experience described simply as 'I am this'. The experience was not quite what he had expected, or even what he had hoped for, but somehow it didn't seem to matter. He was home.

The question now arose, who was Nick going to tell? The world had not changed. People were still accepting the emotional pain as normal and would even argue to justify it when questioned. No, Nick had found the answer to the universe and to questions such as 'Who am I?' and yet could only carry on with his everyday life as if nothing had happened. And what had happened? He had only realised what he was and had always been. Nothing had changed. He had nothing to offer to people who wanted to be emotional, and nothing to offer to people looking for experience. He could only share the knowledge and experience of realising one's true nature: I am this.